The US Congress

Christopher J. Bailey

Basil Blackwell

Copyright © Christopher J. Bailey 1989

First published 1989

Basil Blackwell Ltd
108 Cowley Road, Oxford, OX4 1JF, UK

Basil Blackwell Inc.
432 Park Avenue South, Suite 1503
New York, NY 10016, USA

British Library Cataloguing in Publication Data
Bailey, Christopher J.
  The US Congress
  1. United States. Congress
  I. Title
  328.73

  ISBN 0–631–15861–8
  ISBN 0–631–15862–6 Pbk

Library of Congress Cataloging in Publication Data
Bailey, Christopher J.
  The US Congress.

  Bibliography: p.
  Includes index.
  1. United States. Congress. I. Title.
JK1061 B296 1989   328.73 88–33303
ISBN 0–631–15861–8
ISBN 0–631–15862–6 (pbk.)

Typeset in 10 on 12 pt Baskerville
by Photo·graphics, Honiton, Devon
Printed in Great Britain by T.J. Press Ltd, Padstow, Cornwall

Contents

List of Tables and Figures

Acknowledgements

It is with pleasure that I take this opportunity to thank the various people who have helped me with this book. First, I should like to thank Sean Magee of Basil Blackwell for offering me the opportunity to write it. The staff at Blackwell have been easy to work with, prompt and efficient. Other publishers would do well to note their example. Gillian Peele and Mike Tappin read much of the manuscript, and offered many suggestions for improvement. Colin Bonwick responded patiently to my many questions about the intentions of the framers of the US Constitution and the early political developments in the new Republic. Martin Crawford introduced me to the world of the British travellers, answered my queries about nineteenth-century America and, perhaps more importantly, allowed me to win the occasional game of pool. More generally, I should like to thank all my colleagues in the Department of American Studies at the University of Keele for providing a congenial atmosphere in which to work. Mrs Karen Harrison and Mrs Maureen Simpkin offered invaluable assistance in preparing the manuscript, and I am indebted to them both. Last but not least, I should like to thank my wife Mandy for her affection, encouragement and forbearance at the hours I have spent sitting in front of the word processor. It is to her that I dedicate this book, with love.

1

Introduction

The purpose of this book is to provide a coherent and systematic study of the US Congress. Although it presents a detailed description of the organization and procedures of both the Senate and the House of Representatives, its approach is analytic rather than purely descriptive. In particular, considerable emphasis has been placed upon treating Congress as a *dynamic* institution whose structure has varied over time. Not only does such an approach avoid the 'legalistic' descriptions found in many studies of institutions, but it also facilitates a greater understanding of *why* the two chambers of Congress are organized in a certain way. In other words, the book attempts to provide a framework for the analysis of Congress. As well as describing how the congressional committee system operates, for example, it also attempts to provide the means to answer fundamental, but often overlooked, questions such as why there is a committee system in Congress in the first place, and why that system has evolved in the way it has. Perhaps most importantly, however, the book attempts to show that the study of institutions is far more interesting than many previous studies have suggested.

As with most studies of national political institutions in the United States, the book begins with an examination of the constitutional design of the US Congress. For the student of Congress the Constitution is important for two broad reasons. First, it lays the foundations of the legislature. The principle of bicameralism (the existence of two chambers) is established, and the requirements for membership of each chamber, together with terms of office, clearly detailed. Second, it defines the external setting of Congress. The position of the legislature *vis-à-vis* the executive, the judiciary and the people is delineated. Knowledge of these constitutional provisions is essential for making sense of the contemporary Congress. Proceeding without them would be like trying to play chess without knowing the rules of the game.

The importance of the basic institutional structure of Congress was well recognized by those who framed the Constitution. At the Federal Convention at Philadelphia in 1787 they examined at considerable length the effect which different institutional arrangements would have on behaviour and policy-making. Despite their efforts, however, the Founding Fathers drafted only the blueprint for the new legislature. Their problem, as Woodrow Wilson noted, in a lecture given to students at Columbia University when he was President of Princeton University,

is that government is not a machine, but a living thing. It falls, not under the theory of the universe, but under the theory of organic life. It is accountable to Darwin, not to Newton. It is modified by its environment, necessitated by its tasks, shaped to its functions by the sheer pressure of life.[1]

Rather than being the result of a theory of government, the structure of Congress has, for the most part, emerged as a consequence of usage and practice. The effect of the Constitution has been to set the guidelines for such developments. Explaining just why Congress has developed in the way it has is a central theme of this book. Not only is it an intellectually stimulating exercise in itself, but it is also vital to any understanding of the contemporary institution.

Institutions such as the US Congress are not immutable; they are created by people to meet certain goals, and may be changed by people, either to improve their performance, or else to meet the demands of new goals.[2] Arrangements such as the committee and party systems, for example, should not be viewed as being preordained but as having evolved to satisfy the interests of the members of the Senate and the House of Representatives. As such interests change so institutional arrangements develop accordingly. Any institution which could not evolve to allow its members to satisfy their interests would soon become redundant. Absolutely central to this analysis is the idea that the goals of its membership provide the key to understanding both the dynamics of congressional development and the structure of the contemporary institution. Examining the goals of the membership of the House and the Senate should be a vital component of any study of Congress.

In an influential study published in 1974, David R. Mayhew suggested that the primary goal of most members of Congress is to gain re-election, and that they structure their activities with this end in mind.[3] Senators and representatives behave in a certain way and support those institutional arrangements which, they believe, will increase their chances of electoral success. In other words, members of Congress possess a set of electoral needs which require satisfying. From this premise it follows that any changes in the electoral environment which generate new electoral needs will result in changes in congressional behaviour, and may lead to demands for the establishment of new institutional arrangements. Changes in the electoral environment may also lead to institutional change in another way. The recruitment process to an institution such as Congress is not neutral; it rewards those individuals who possess certain political skills. As the recruitment process changes in response to factors such as the generational replacement of the electorate, the emergence of new issues or the development of new technology, so the political skills necessary for success in the electoral environment also change. The result will be the election of a new generation of legislators with different political skills than their predecessors: they may be less well disposed towards authority, unwilling to compromise, more individualistic. Such generational changes may lead to changes in congressional behaviour and a frustration with existing institutional arrangements. In short, as well as generating a new set of electoral needs, changes in the recruitment process may also lead to the election of legislators with new political skills. Institutional change occurs when these new needs and skills are accommodated.

Having established a framework which facilitates an understanding both of congressional behaviour and institutional arrangements, this book then proceeds to analyse the contemporary Congress. The importance of the recruitment process is recognized in chapter 4 which examines the electoral environment. After describing the basic structure of congressional elections, the more complex aspects of the recruitment process are studied. Particular emphasis is placed upon ascertaining which political skills are currently necessary for electoral success. Central to the argument of this study is the thesis that the traditional role of the political parties in election campaigns has largely been taken over by candidate-centred campaign organizations. In other words, candidates are in most instances self-selected; they raise their own funds and determine their own campaign strategies with the help of hired consultants. Such an environment rewards different political skills and generates far different electoral needs than one in which the parties play a greater role.

More detail about the qualities required for success in the highly competitive and volatile electoral environment of the 1970s and the 1980s is then provided in chapter 5 which discusses the stability and nature of Congress's membership. Both these factors are pertinent to an understanding of the manner in which the institution functions. Just as changes in the nature of Congress's membership may lead to demands for institutional reform, so changes in the stability of the membership may themselves undermine existing rules and procedures. Quite simply, membership instability may cause institutional instability. What emerges from this study of Congress's membership is that recent years have seen significant changes in both the background of senators and representatives, and the rate of turnover in the two chambers. Members are not only younger and more politically inexperienced than their predecessors but, until very recently, the overall level of membership stability had also declined. Such changes have had an effect on almost every aspect of the institution's structure and activities: from the way members cast their votes to patterns of activity to the way the committees operate to changes in floor procedures.

An analysis of those factors which influence the way a representative or senator casts his or her vote on an issue is, in fact, a useful means of illustrating the effect that changes in the electoral environment have had on congressional behaviour. In particular, the development of the candidate-centred campaign organization, together with the increased uncertainty about the chances of gaining re-election, have led members of Congress to pay far more attention to what they believe to be the wishes of their constituents when casting their votes. This fact underpins the relationship of the individual member with the other main actors in the legislative process: the political parties, interest groups and the President. Although all these actors may attempt to influence roll call behaviour their ability to do so is limited by the member's desire to please his or her constituents and thus gain re-election. The influx of members who owe their electoral success to their own efforts, not to the efforts of the political parties, interest groups or the President, means that legislative coalitions have to be painstakingly negotiated. Votes can not be expected as matter of course.

Roll call voting is not the only aspect of congressional behaviour to be affected by the primacy of constituency politics. The need to cater to constituency interests has also affected the type of activity performed by members of Congress. In the modern Congress far more resources and time are devoted to the provision of what might be termed 'constituency services' than had previously been the case. Staff have been redeployed to state and district offices, more casework is being done, and individual senators and representatives are spending far more time in their constituencies. This reordering of the individual member's priorities has clearly affected the legislative function of Congress. Not only is legislation scanned for its domestic implications, but less time is available for law-making. One result of this development is the apparent inability of Congress to respond to the challenges and problems generated by the large budget deficit in the United States. The legislative function of Congress has also been undermined by the institution's increasing concern with oversight. Promoted initially by the revelations of misdemeanours by the Executive Branch which emerged in the wake of Watergate and the Vietnam War, oversight has come to take up a significant proportion of Congress's time and resources. Congress's capacity to conduct oversight has been strengthened through a number of reforms, more committee hearings are held, and more staff assigned to the task of evaluating the performance of the Executive Branch.

The changes in Congress's activity which are detailed in this book are best understood by reference to the changing priorities of its membership as the requirements for electoral success have altered. Members have increasingly regarded a concern for their constituencies as essential for their continued survival in office, while a new generation of senators and representatives elected in the wake of Vietnam and Watergate found that attacks on the activities of the Executive Branch were a useful political issue. The changing priorities of the membership are not only of use in explaining changes in congressional activity or roll call behaviour, however, they are also the key to understanding changes in the structure of Congress. Without some knowledge of the changed priorities of the membership recent developments in the committee systems, floor procedures and leadership of both the House and the Senate would be difficult to comprehend.

Long recognized as being at the heart of Congress's operations, the committee system has developed over the years as the demands of the membership of the House and Senate have changed. Not only has this process led to the creation and abolition of panels, as new policy areas have been added to the public agenda and others removed, but it has also generated changes in the internal structure of the committees. During the 1970s, for example, pressure from a new generation of senators and representatives led to significant reforms in the methods by which members were assigned to committees, the means by which the chairmen were chosen and the role which junior members were able to play in the committees' activities. An important component of the latter was a proliferation and institutionalization of subcommittees: a development which caused some commentators to talk about 'subcommittee government' in Congress.[4] Although such developments provided junior members with the means to play an active role in the policy process, the net result was to fragment power within the two chambers. In short, the committee system was adapted to meet the changing needs of the membership as a more volatile and competitive electoral environment placed a premium upon the early acquisition of resources.

A similar pattern of changing membership needs generating institutional reform can also be observed in the floor procedures of the Senate and the House of Representatives. Over the years these have been adapted and refined to meet new demands. In the late nineteenth century, for example, the right of the majority to control the proceedings of the House of Representatives was confirmed when the chamber accepted various rulings by Speaker Thomas Reed aimed at restricting the ability of the minority to obstruct legislation. More recently, the majority has reasserted its authority by reining in the power of the Rules Committee. In the Senate, recent developments have seen changes in both the use of the filibuster or the methods by which members may obstruct legislation and the use of amendments. Such developments are important because procedures have a direct impact upon policy. With its many opportunities to block legislation, the legislative process in Congress tends to produce general 'goal-orientated' bills which are clearly the result of the compromises necessary to gain their passage.

One of the primary functions of party leaders in a system with multiple veto points is to provide some coherence so that institutional difficulties may be overcome. In Congress the problem for the leadership is that, apart from the Speaker of the House of Representatives, they have too few resources to meet their responsibilities. Always conscious of their own needs and prerogatives, the membership of the House and Senate have generally been unwilling to cede authority to the party leaders. As with the committee system and floor procedures, the patterns of leadership in the two chambers reflect the requirements of the membership. In recent years, the nature of the prevailing electoral environment has served to limit the authority of the party leaders. Electoral politics of the 1980s have tended to promote individualism rather than collective action.

Having provided both a framework for the study of Congress, and a description of the institution, this book concludes with a short chapter which assesses the role of Congress in the contemporary American political system. In particular, it raises a series of questions concerning both the way in which Congress operates and the purpose of a legislature in a modern political system. Finally, for the benefit of those wishing to follow up any of the points raised in the book, a fairly comprehensive bibliography of major works is included at the end of the book.

Notes

1 Woodrow Wilson *Constitutional Government in the United States* (New York, Columbia University Press, 1911), p. 56.
2 Armen A. Alchian 'Uncertainty, Evolution, and Economic Theory' *Journal of Political Economy* (58:3), 1950, pp. 211–21.
3 David R. Mayhew *Congress: The Electoral Connection* (New Haven, Yale University Press, 1974).
4 Roger H. Davidson 'Subcommittee Government: New Channels for Policy Making' in Thomas E. Mann and Norman J. Ornstein eds *The New Congress* (Washington DC, American Enterprise Institute, 1981), pp. 99–133.

2

The Constitutional Framework

Defending the US Constitution in *Federalist* (51), James Madison made clear the importance which the Founding Fathers attached to the national legislature when he wrote: 'In republican government, the legislative authority necessarily predominates.'[1] Madison's view of the primacy of the legislature echoed the seventeenth-century English philosopher John Locke's assertion that: '[the] legislature . . . is the supreme power of the commonwealth.'[2] It was Congress, not the Presidency, which was regarded as the central element of the new political system, and both the proceedings of the Federal Convention of 1787 and the written Constitution which emerged from these deliberations, reflected this fact. Not only were the debates at Philadelphia dominated by discussions about the structure and role that the national legislature should perform, but approximately half the new Constitution was devoted to providing details of this institution. The length of these considerations once again reflected the advice of John Locke that: 'the first and fundamental positive law of all commonwealths is the establishing of the legislative power.'[3] To this extent, the constitutional design of Congress was much more explicit than that of the other institutions of government. Unlike the Presidency, for example, the *basic* structure and powers of Congress were delineated reasonably clearly in the Constitution, and established distinct boundaries governing the future development of the institution.

THE STRUCTURE OF CONGRESS

The basic structure of Congress – the creation of the House of Representatives and the Senate – was decided at a very early stage of the Federal Convention. From the outset it was generally agreed that the national legislature should be bicameral, and both the Randolph and Pinckney Plans, laid before the Convention on its first working day, provided for a two-chambered legislature. Two days later, James Madison, a delegate from Virginia, recorded that 'The Third Resolution "that the national legislature ought to consist of two branches" was agreed to without debate or dissent, except that of Pennsylvania, given probably from complaisance to Doctor Franklin who was understood to be partial to a single House of Legislation'.[4] Not only did twelve of the thirteen states already have bicameral legislatures, a fact which led George Mason of Virginia to suggest that 'an attachment to more than one branch in the legislature' was one of the two points on which 'the mind of the people of America . . . was well settled', but dividing power between two chambers was also regarded as a means of countering the threat of a legislative tyranny.[5]

The possibility of 'legislative despotism' was raised at the Federal Convention by James Wilson, a delegate from Pennsylvania. He argued that:

If the Legislative authority be not restrained, there can be neither liberty nor stability; and it can only be restrained by dividing it within itself, into distinct and independent branches. In a single House there is no check, but the inadequate one, of the virtue and good sense of those who compose it.[6]

This theme was taken up and developed in *Federalist* by James Madison who argued that the best way of countering the likelihood of any abuse of power by the legislature was to: 'divide the legislature into different branches; and to render them, by different modes of election and different principles of action, as little connected with each other as the nature of their common functions and their common dependence on society will admit'.[7] Together, these statements by Wilson and Madison clearly articulate the basic principles of bicameralism: that the legislature should be composed of two 'distinct and independent' chambers, and that these chambers should somehow be 'different' from one another.

Having accepted the idea of bicameralism and reinforced it by passing a resolution allowing either chamber to originate laws, the Founding Fathers then proceeded to discuss how the two houses of Congress should be constituted. Particularly important in this respect were their deliberations regarding the mode of election for each body. Factors such as the requirements needed to stand for office, the method of choosing legislators, and the frequency of elections are among the most important determinants of the character of the legislature. They help to shape, for example, both the nature of the legislature's membership, and the overall level of membership stability. In deciding upon a specific mode of electing each chamber, therefore, the Founding Fathers were making clear their expectations about the future nature and role of the House of Representatives and the Senate.

The House of Representatives

The Fourth Resolution of the Randolph Plan provided that 'the first branch of the National Legislature' – the House of Representatives – 'ought to be elected by the people of the several States.' This proposal was bitterly attacked by Roger Sherman of Connecticut and Elbridge Gerry of Massachusetts. Both suggested that the general populace lacked the requisite information to make decisions and were thus liable to be misled by demagogues. 'The people', Sherman declared, 'should have as little to do as may be about the Government. They want information and are constantly liable to be misled.'[8] Gerry concurred with Sherman, arguing that: 'The people do not want virtue, but are the dupes of pretended patriots . . . it has been fully confirmed by experience that they are daily misled into the most baneful measures and opinions by the false reports circulated by designing men.'[9] Rather than being popularly elected, Sherman and Gerry proposed that the first branch be elected by the state legislatures. This proposal was strongly opposed by George Mason who argued that the House of Representatives ought to be 'the grand repository of the democratic principle of the Government. It was, so to speak, to be our House of Commons – It ought to know and sympathise with every part of the community.'[10] Mason's assertions about the need for direct elections were supported by James Wilson who contended that: 'No government could long subsist without the confidence of the people' and by James Madison who considered 'the popular election of one branch of the National Legislature as essential to every plan of free government.'[11] After much debate the principle that the House of Representatives should be elected by popular ballot was accepted in two separate votes: one on the 31 May 1787 and the other on the 6 June 1787.

The eventual choice of direct, popular elections as the mode of electing the House of Representatives was predicated on the assumption that the chamber should be the 'grand repository' of democracy. This notion was further reflected in the fact that representatives were only given two-year terms. As Madison wrote in *Federalist* (52):

it is essential to liberty that the government in general should have a common interest with the people, so it is particularly essential that the branch of it under consideration should have an immediate dependence on, and an intimate sympathy with, the people. Frequent elections are unquestionably the only policy by which this dependence and sympathy can be effectively secured.[12]

From this and other remarks it is apparent that the House of Representatives was designed as a *representative* institution. Its most important function was to represent and regulate the various interests and concerns in American society. In his celebrated *Federalist* (10) Madison makes plain his belief that this function is central to the work of a legislature: 'The regulation of these various and interfering interests forms the principal task of modern legislation and involves the spirit of party and faction in the necessary and ordinary operations of government.'[13] The very purpose of legislation is thus intimately linked by Madison to the idea of representation.

The Senate

Having decided that the main role of the House of Representatives was to provide a forum for the various interests in American society, the problem then faced by the Founding Fathers was to determine what role the Senate should play in the new political system. Some expected it to become an advisory council to the President; this after all had usually been the function of second chambers in the various colonial governments.[14] Others, with Shay's rebellion over taxation fresh in their minds, expected it to be a guardian of the 'commercial and monied interest'.[15] The prevailing sentiment at the Federal Convention, however, was that the chamber should perform two main functions. First, it was argued that the Senate should act as a check on the popularly elected House of Representatives. The House of Representatives was acknowledged to be 'the grand repository of the democratic principle of the government', but was also thought likely to possess certain weaknesses, or deficiencies, endemic to large, popularly elected legislatures: tendencies to instability, to volatile, inconsistent, erratic decision-making, and to a short-term view of good public policy. The Senate, it was felt, should provide a moderating, stabilizing counterweight: should be the source of a more considered, more experienced, long-term view of good public policy. As James Madison stated: 'The use of the Senate is to consist in its proceeding with more coolness, with more system, and with more wisdom, than the popular branch'.[16] This theme was developed by Madison in *Federalist* (63):

there are particular moments in public affairs when the people, stimulated by some irregular passion, or some illicit advantage, or misled by the artful misrepresentations of interested men, may call for measures which they themselves will afterwards be the most ready to lament and condemn. In these critical moments, how salutary will be the interference of some temperate and respectable body of citizens, in order to check the misguided career, and to suspend the blow meditated by the people against themselves, until reason, justice, and truth can regain their authority and the public mind.[17]

The second function of the chamber was to act as a guardian of the interests of the states, and to protect them against encroachment by the Federal

Government. In part, the Founding Fathers were merely bowing to the political realities of the day in ascribing this role to the Senate. Somehow they had to persuade the people of the thirteen quasi-independent states that their interests would be safeguarded in the new system of government. This point was made at the Convention by George Mason who argued that:

The state legislatures . . . ought to have some means of defending themselves against encroachments by the National Government. In every other department we have studiously endeavoured to provide for its self-defence. Shall we leave the States alone unprovided with the means for this purpose? And what better means can we provide than the giving them some share in, or rather, to make them a constituent part of the National Government.[18]

Essentially, the Senate was given what might be termed a restraining function. A major part of its responsibility was to curb any abuse of power by the House of Representatives or the Federal Government in general.

The Senate's role as a protector of the rights of the states and as a check on the House of Representatives was reflected in both the unanimous decision to have senators selected by the state legislatures rather than by popular election, and in the fact that senators were given six-year terms with only one-third up for re-election at any one time.[19] While the latter helped distance the Senate from the 'passions of the electorate' and promote stability, the former arrangement, as Madison stated, was 'recommended by the double advantage of favoring a select appointment, and of giving to the State governments such an agency in the formation of the federal government as must secure the authority of the former, and may form a convenient link between the two systems'.[20] It was thought that selection by the state legislatures would result in a more distinguished membership: a point which was reinforced by the fact that senators had to be over thirty years old, compared with the age requirement of twenty-five years for representatives.

While the decision to have senators selected by the state legislatures was generally agreed, the question of the numerical representation of the states in the Senate was far more controversial and almost led to the breakdown of the Convention. The small states, led by Oliver Ellsworth of Connecticut, demanded equal representation in the Congress as the price of union, while delegates from the larger states, with the exception of James Madison, argued that the states should be represented according to population. Madison argued against weighted representations, believing that it would make the Senate far too large, and consequently prone to the same deficiencies as the House of Representatives. Finally, after a great deal of debate, a compromise solution to this problem was reached which provided for weighted representation in the House of Representatives, but equal representation in the Senate. Representatives were apportioned according to the size of a state's population, with one representative for every 30,000 inhabitants, and each state was given two senators.

Implicit in the Founding Fathers' creation of two chambers with different constituencies, size of membership, and terms of office, was a belief that these structural differences would generate different patterns of behaviour. As Richard F. Fenno has written: 'the superior "coolness", "system", and "wisdom" of the Senate, for example, were assumed to flow from its smaller size, the longer terms of its members, and their election by state legislatures.'[21] While the validity of these assumptions about the likely behaviour of the House of Representatives and the Senate may be questioned, they are important in understanding why certain powers were given to one chamber and not the other.

THE POWERS OF CONGRESS

Both the general powers granted to Congress and the specific prerogatives conferred on the House of Representatives and the Senate clearly reflect the various functions which the Founding Fathers expected the two chambers, either singularly or collectively, to perform. First and foremost among these functions, and the *raison d'être* of the Federal Convention of 1787, was 'to form a more perfect Union'. When John Randolph of Virginia opened the main business of the Convention on the 29 May 1787, he did so by listing what he regarded as the defects of the Articles of Confederation under which the country had been governed since 1781. He argued:

First, that the confederation produced no security against foreign invasion; congress not being permitted to prevent a war nor support it by their own authority. Secondly, that the federal government could not check the quarrels between the states . . .Thirdly, that there were many advantages, which the United States might acquire, which were not attainable under the confederation – such as a productive impost – counteraction of the commercial regulations of other nations – pushing of commerce – etc. Fourthly, that the federal government could not defend itself against the incroachments of the states.[22]

At the heart of the Founding Fathers' reservations about the Articles of Confederation was a belief that the existing Continental Congress, which had no power to raise taxes and was thus wholly dependent upon the states, was too weak. It was thought that a strong national legislature was essential if the United States was to be prevented from disintegrating.[23]

General Powers

The general powers granted to Congress in Article I, Section 8 of the Constitution were intended to strengthen the national legislature and, indeed, many of these powers were explicitly designed to remedy the 'defects' mentioned by Randolph. Congress, for example, was given the power to raise taxes, to regulate commerce, to coin money, to declare war and to raise an army and navy. To ensure that these grants of power would be effective, the last clause of this Section of the Constitution states that Congress shall have the power 'to make all Laws which shall be necessary and proper for carrying into Execution the foregoing powers, and all other Powers vested by this Constitution in the Government of the United States, or in any Department of Officer thereof'. Without the *necessary and proper* clause Madison believed that 'the whole constitution would be a dead letter'.[24] The authority of the national legislature over the state governments was further enhanced by the provisions of Article I, Section 10 of the Constitution which prohibited the individual states from coining money, introducing import or export duties and entering into alliances with foreign nations. Finally, the supremacy of federal law over state law was confirmed by Article VI of the Constitution which stated that: 'This Constitution, and the laws of the United States which shall be made in Pursuance thereof . . . shall be the Supreme Law of the Land.'

While the provisions of Article I, Sections 8 and 10, and Article VI established the *legislative* power of the national legislature, other aspects of the Constitution gave Congress the authority to check or *oversee* the other branches of the Federal Government. Article I, Sections 2 and 3 enabled Congress to remove federal officials from office by a vote of impeachment by the House of Representatives and a vote of conviction by the Senate. Article III, Section 2 allowed Congress, except in the circumstances noted by the Constitution, to determine the 'appellate Jurisdiction' of the Supreme Court.[25] In addition to the general powers contained in these clauses, the Constitution also gave specific oversight powers to the House of Representatives and the Senate. In particular, the House of Representatives was given the 'power of the purse' while the right to vet executive appointments and ratify treaties was conferred on the Senate.

Specific Powers

As the institution of the Federal Government most sensitive to popular sentiment the House of Representatives, in Article I, Section 7, was granted the prerogative of initiating all legislation regarding taxes. James Madison, writing in *Federalist* (58), argued that the power which this particular right bestowed was enormous:

The House of Representatives cannot only refuse, but they alone can propose the supplies requisite for the support of the government. They, in a word, hold the purse – that powerful instrument by which we behold, in the history of the British Constitution, an infant and humble representation of the people gradually enlarging the sphere of its activity and importance, and finally reducing, as far as it seems to have wished, all the overgrown prerogatives of the other branches of government. This power may, in fact, be regarded as the most complete and effectual weapon with which any constitution can arm the immediate representatives of the people, for obtaining a redress of every grievance, and for carrying into effect every just and salutary measure.[26]

In other words, Madison believed that the 'power of the purse' provided the House of Representatives with the means of controlling the other institutions of government. To reinforce this power Article I, Section 9 of the Constitution stated that: 'No money shall be drawn from the Treasury, but in Consequence of Appropriations made by Law.' Using more simple language in *Federalist* (48), Madison noted that: 'the legislature alone has access to the pockets of the people.'[27]

The House of Representatives was given the 'power of the purse' because it was regarded by the Founding Fathers as the institution which most embodied the 'democratic principle'. In much the same manner specific oversight powers were granted to the Senate on the basis of certain predictions about the likely nature of that institution. On the assumption that the qualifications necessary to become a senator and the method of electing the chamber would ensure a highly experienced, knowledgeable membership, the Senate was given a number of executive functions. Article II, Section 2 of the Constitution, for example, gave the Senate both the right to confirm the President's appointment of 'Ambassadors, other public Ministers and Consuls, Judges of the Supreme Court, and all other officers of the United States', and the right to ratify treaties. Discussing the latter power in *Federalist* (64) John Jay made plain the reason why the Senate was given a role in foreign policy:

As the select assemblies for choosing the President, as well as the State legislatures who appoint the senators, will in general be composed of the most enlightened and respectable citizens, there is reason to presume that their attention and their votes will be directed to those men who have become distinguished by their abilities and virtue . . . the President and senators so chosen will always be of the number of those who best understand our national interests . . . With such men the power of making treaties may be safely lodged.[28]

From this and other observations it is clear that the oversight functions of the Senate were predicated upon the belief that the chamber would possess certain qualities. It was given responsibilities in precisely those areas where it was felt that the advice and consent of a 'capable set of men' would be most needed.

Limits on Power

Derived from the Founding Fathers' conception of the role of the national legislature in their new political system, the powers granted to Congress by the Constitution were substantial, and included not only legislative but also executive and judicial functions. These powers, however, were not unlimited. Article I, Section 9 of the Constitution, for example, places eight specific limitations on Congress's power. In addition to limitations on Congress's power to regulate the slave trade, grant titles of nobility, tax and appropriate funds, the Constitution prohibits *bills of attainder* which declare a person guilty of a crime without a trial, and *ex post facto laws* which make an action a crime after it has been committed. Madison argued that the latter two prohibitions, in particular, constituted a 'constitutional bulwark in favour of personal security and private rights'.[29] Congressional power is further limited by the first ten amendments to the Constitution, known as the 'Bill of Rights'. The First Amendment prohibits Congress from establishing a state religion or preventing free speech, press or assembly. Other amendments protect the right of property, fair trial and freedom from arbitrary arrest. Although the Constitution does not explicitly state who should interpret these constitutional restraints, this function has been performed by the Supreme Court since 1803 when Chief Justice John Marshall declared in *Marbury v. Madison* that 'it is emphatically the province and duty of the judicial department to say what the law is'. This assertion of judicial review enabled the Court to declare 106 Acts of Congress unconstitutional, and therefore invalid, between 1789 and 1983.[30]

The final constraint upon congressional power is the system of 'checks and balances' which are built into the political system. Not only did the creation of a bicameral legislature mean that legislation had to pass through two distinct chambers, but the legislative process itself is divided between Congress and the President. Article II, Section 3 of the Constitution allows the President 'to convene both Houses, or either of them'. The President is also permitted to 'recommend to their Consideration such Measures as he shall judge necessary and expedient'. Perhaps the most important power which the President possesses, however, is the power of the veto. Article I, Section 7 allows the President to veto a bill or resolution passed by Congress. To override a presidential veto, a two-thirds vote is required in both chambers. In *Federalist* (73) Alexander Hamilton argued that the veto power:

not only serves as a shield to the executive, but it furnishes an additional security against the enaction of improper laws. It establishes a salutary check upon the legislative body, calculated to guard the community against the effects of faction, precipitancy, or any impulse unfriendly to the public good, which may happen to influence a majority of that body.[31]

By involving the President in the legislative process the Founding Fathers added another restriction to Congress's power. They also ensured that there would be a dynamic tension between the two branches of government: as Madison stated in *Federalist* (51) 'Ambition must be made to counteract ambition.'[32]

AN INCOMPLETE SYSTEM

It is clear that the Constitution places considerable limits on Congress's power. Writing in *Federalist* (52) James Madison stated that: 'the federal legislature will possess a part only, of that supreme legislative authority which is vested completely in the British Parliament.'[33] This fact was noted almost 100 years later by Lord Bryce, who informed his readers that: 'Congress is not like the Parliament of England . . . a sovereign assembly, but is subject to the Constitution.'[34] Its powers, and the limits on those powers, are delineated in the Constitution. Although the structure and powers of Congress were far more clearly specified in the Constitution than any other office in the federal system, there is a sense in which Woodrow Wilson in his classic work *Congressional Government* was correct to state that:

The Constitution itself is not a complete system; it takes none but the first steps in organisation . . . it grants specifically enumerated powers of legislation to a representative Congress, outlining the organisation of the two houses of that body and definitely providing for the election of its members, whose numbers it regulates and the conditions of whose choice it names.[35]

The Constitution, for example, makes little reference to leadership within Congress. Article I, Section 2 states that: 'The House of Representatives shall chuse their Speaker and other Officers' and Article I, Section 3 states that: 'The Vice President shall be President of the Senate, but shall have no vote, unless they be equally divided' and that 'The Senate shall chuse their other Officers, and also a President *Pro Tempore*, in the absence of the Vice President, or when he shall exercise the Office of President of the United States' but makes no further comment on their powers. Moreover, the Constitution makes no reference to either the role of the political parties or committees within Congress. Such details are deliberately left to Congress to determine. As Article I, Section 5 of the Constitution states: 'Each House may determine the Rules of its Proceedings.' Overall, as Woodrow Wilson points out, the Constitution generates a general 'framework' for Congress which sets the guidelines of its future development. Such development, however, can only be understood by reference to factors outside the Constitution itself.

Notes

1 James Madison *Federalist* (51) in Alexander Hamilton, James Madison and John Jay *The Federalist Papers* ed. Max Beloff (Oxford, Basil Blackwell, 1987), p. 265.
2 John Locke *Two Treatises of Government* (London, Everyman 1984 edn), p. 183.
3 Ibid.
4 James Madison *The Debates in the Federal Convention of 1787* eds Gaillard Hunt and James Brown Scott (Oxford, Oxford University Press, 1920), p. 31.
5 Ibid. p. 135. Mason believed that the other point on which Americans seemed to agree was 'an attachment to Republican Government'.
6 Ibid. p. 109.
7 Madison *Federalist* (51), pp. 265–6.
8 Madison *The Debates*, pp. 31–2.
9 Ibid. p. 32.
10 Ibid.
11 Ibid. pp. 32–3.
12 Madison *Federalist* (52), pp. 269–70.
13 Madison *Federalist* (10), p. 43.
14 See Jackson Turner Main *The Upper House in Revolutionary America 1763–1788* (Madison, University of Wisconsin Press, 1967).
15 See Madison *The Debates*, pp. 70, 73.
16 Ibid. p. 71.
17 Madison *Federalist* (63), p. 323.
18 Madison *The Debates*, p. 74.
19 The Seventeenth Amendment (1913) provided for the direct election of senators.
20 Madison *Federalist* (62), p. 316.
21 Richard F. Fenno *The United States Senate: A Bicameral Perspective* (Washington DC, American Enterprise Institute, 1982), p. 4.
22 Madison *The Debates*, p. 23.
23 See Edmund Morgan 'Safety in Numbers: Madison, Hume, and the Tenth *Federalist*' *Huntington Library Quarterly* (Spring), 1986, p. 101.
24 Madison *Federalist* (44), p. 229.
25 The 'exceptions clause' has, in fact, rarely been invoked because an attempt to do so is usually regarded as an attack on the 'separation of powers'. For a useful discussion of this subject see US Senate, Committee on the Judiciary, Subcommittee on the Constitution, *Hearings*, 'Constitutional Restraints Upon the Judiciary', 97th Congress, 1st sess. 20, 21 May and 22 June 1981.
26 Madison *Federalist* (58), pp. 299–300.

27 Madison *Federalist* (48), p. 254.
28 John Jay *Federalist* (64) in Alexander Hamilton, James Madison and John Jay *The Federalist Papers* ed. Max Beloff (Oxford, Basil Blackwell, 1987), p. 329.
29 Madison *Federalist* (44), p. 228.
30 Roger H. Davidson and Walter J. Oleszek *Congress and its Members* (Washington DC, Congressional Quarterly Press, 1985), p. 23.
31 Alexander Hamilton *Federalist* (73) in Alexander Hamilton, James Madison and John Jay *The Federalist Papers* ed. Max Beloff (Oxford, Basil Blackwell, 1987), pp. 375–6.
32 Madison *Federalist* (51), p. 265.
33 Madison *Federalist* (52), p. 272.
34 James Bryce *The American Commonwealth* (London, Macmillan, 1891), p. 186.
35 Woodrow Wilson *Congressional Government* (London, Constable, 1914), p. 8.

3

The Dynamics of Congressional Change

Although the Founding Fathers did not attempt to provide a detailed blueprint for Congress's internal structure, the provisions of the Constitution have tended to generate a general framework governing the organization of the institution. Constitutional differences in size, membership and terms of office between the House of Representatives and the Senate, for example, have been reflected in slightly different structures and procedures in the two chambers. While the House of Representatives has tended to be hierarchical and rule-bound, the Senate, because of its smaller size and its constitutional design as 'an instrument for preserving the residual sovereignty' left to the states, has tended to be egalitarian and flexible.[1] As each senator is regarded as an ambassador from a 'sovereign' state he or she is usually granted more respect than a representative from a small district within a state, and as a small institution the Senate can afford to be more relaxed in its procedures than the much larger House of Representatives. Hence the Senate's traditions of unlimited debate and an open amending process, and the central role of the Rules Committee in the proceedings of the House.[2] More graphically, the rules of the modern Senate are contained in approximately 90 pages while more than 400 pages are needed to describe those of the House of Representatives.

Within the broad structural framework established by the constitutional design of Congress the specific organization of each chamber has varied over time as the institution has responded to the changing nature of the United States. The House of the 1980s, for example, differs considerably from that of the nineteenth century, or even the mid-twentieth century in terms of its rules, partisan behaviour and workload. Similarly, Senate practices, procedures and output have also changed over time.[3] Often overlooked by many studies of Congress, which have tended to be 'time-bound' in their approach, the question of *why* such change occurs is very important. By answering this question it is possible to develop a better understanding of both the structure and organization of the contemporary Congress, and the way in which the institution interacts with its environment.

ADAPTIVE AND CONSOLIDATIVE CHANGE

In their study of structural innovation in the House of Representatives, Roger H. Davidson and Walter J. Oleszek suggest that congressional change has two sources: pressures emanating from the *external* environment, and *internal* pressures arising from the goals of individual congressmen.[4] The former dictates the extent and type of workload with which the House of Representatives has to deal and fashions its relationship with the other institutions of government, while the latter primarily determines how power will be distributed in the chamber. In order to survive, it is argued, an institution like the House of Representatives must both *adapt* to changes in its external environment, to changes in the role of government and the public agenda, and relieve internal stresses caused by membership changes through what are termed *consolidative* innovations. The Legislative Reorganization Acts of 1946 and 1970 which overhauled the congressional committee systems, and the Congressional Budget and Impoundment Act of 1974 which enhanced Congress's role in the budget process, are given as examples of adaptive change, while changes in the seniority system, particularly those which gave junior congressmen more prestigious committee appointments, are cited as examples of consolidation.

It would appear, therefore, that the specific organization of the House of Representatives and the Senate at any given time should be viewed as the product of their constitutional design, and the external and internal demands placed upon each chamber. As the role of the national government increased during the nineteenth century, for example, so the operation and procedures of Congress changed as the institution adjusted to new circumstances.[5] Perhaps the most visible sign of this adjustment was the emergence of a complex committee system, and the development of a centralized leadership structure in both the House of Representatives and the Senate.

New External Demands

For the first eight or nine Congresses, both the House of Representatives and the Senate dealt with legislation either in a 'committee of the whole' or in short-lived special or select committees. This situation began to change in around 1810 when the pressures generated by western expansion, an increase in interstate and international trade, and the Anglo-American War of 1812 resulted in new demands being placed upon the federal government and stimulated committee growth in Congress.[6] Between 1810 and 1825 the number of standing committees in the House increased from nine to twenty-eight. In the Senate the use of standing committees was finally accepted in 1816 when twelve were created. So quickly did the committee system develop that one British observer writing in 1833 was able to state that: 'The business of Congress is almost always prepared by permanent committees.'[7] As the national agenda further expanded in the second half of the nineteenth century so the number of standing committees also increased. Between 1861 and 1913 the number of committees in the House increased from thirty-nine to sixty, and the number in the Senate from twenty-two to seventy-four.[8]

A strong, centralized leadership structure also developed rapidly in both chambers during this period. In the 1890s both the Republican organization of Senators William B. Allison (Republican, Iowa) and Nelson W. Aldrich (Republican, Rhode Island), and the Democratic organization of Senator Arthur P. Gorman (Democratic, Maryland) began to use the party caucus to control standing committee assignments and the scheduling of business in the Senate. Aldrich has since gained the reputation as having been the most powerful senator in the history of the chamber.[9] Similarly, under Speakers John G. Carlisle (1883–9), Thomas Reed (1889–91 and 1895–9), Charles F. Crisp (1891–5) and Joseph Cannon (1903–10) power in the House of Representatives was centralized to an unprecedented degree. These four Speakers used their right to recognize members on the floor of the chamber, and to refer bills to committees, to establish considerable control over the proceedings of the House. Interestingly, both Senator Aldrich and Speaker Cannon used after-hours poker games to further their control over their respective institutions. At these sessions, legislative tactics were discussed, committee assignments decided and the loyalty of lieutenants cemented.

New Internal Demands

The growth of Congress's committee system and the development of strong leadership in the late nineteenth century has in the past been viewed as a product of the external demands placed upon the institution. Equally significant as a cause of institutional change, however, was a transformation in the membership of Congress. For almost 100 years both the House of Representatives and the Senate experienced considerable difficulty in holding on to their members who frequently left Congress for other opportunities, both governmental and private. Five of the original twenty-six senators resigned before serving their full terms of office, and of the ninety-four senators who served between 1789 and 1801, thirty-three resigned before completing their terms.[10] Although desertion from the House in this period was not quite so bad, approximately 6 per cent of all representatives resigned at the end of each Congress. Of the 465 representatives who left Congress between 1811 and 1820 only forty-nine were defeated at the polls.[11] The attitudes of many were summed up by one representative who wrote in a letter home that his service in the House had 'produced in me nothing but an absolute loathing and disgust'.[12]

One cause of the disquiet among the early members of Congress was the city of Washington itself. Chosen as the site of the national government as a concession to the southern states, the city had little to recommend it. One observer writing in the 1830s noted that: 'The Capitol . . . and the White-house . . . are the only two specimens of architecture in the whole town; the rest being mere hovels'.[13] Another traveller, writing twenty years later, expressed his disappointment with the city: 'it looks like a big village whose wide streets were built Lord knows for whom or what'.[14] Physical discomfort, however, was only part of the reason for the flight from the early Congress. Not only was Washington DC – half-built, humid, and infested with mosquitoes – less pleasant than Philadelphia or New York, but, equally significant, political life centred on the states rather than the federal government. The state governments, not the government in Washington DC, were responsible for most domestic policy during this period. This fact was noted by one British traveller of the period who observed:

The truth, I believe, is, that the American Congress have really very little to do. All the multiplied details of municiple legislation fall within the province of the State governments, and the regulation of commerce and foreign intercourse practically includes all the important questions which they are called to decide.[15]

The prestige of the early Senate, for example, was little more than that of a high state office.[16] It was only during the second half of the nineteenth century, as the growth of the federal government and the increased importance of the slavery question made a career in Congress more attractive, that this pattern began to change. In both chambers membership began to stabilize, and the average length of service began to increase.[17]

These changes in congressional career patterns had a profound effect on the organization and structure of Congress. Indeed, they were a prime cause of the transformation of the House of Representatives from a debating chamber to a 'professional organization' at the end of the nineteenth century.[18] Not only did the lower level of membership turnover generate a fairly stable environment, and thus facilitate the development of procedures such as the seniority system which rewarded longevity, but the new generation of 'professional' congressmen had different needs and incentives than their predecessors. As professional politicians one of their main requirements was the establishment of a predictable career structure. Like many of their counterparts in industry and the civil service they sought the comfort of institutionalized patterns of promotion and prestige. To gain these benefits they demanded changes in the institution's existing practices.

RECRUITMENT PRACTICES

The 'institutionalization' of both the House of Representatives and the Senate towards the end of the nineteenth century can therefore be explained by reference to a number of external and internal pressures acting upon the institution. A further refinement of this analysis can be made, however, by examining in more detail the precise nature of the needs and incentives of congressmen. A number of studies have suggested that the primary goal of most incumbent politicians is to gain re-election, and that they tend to organize their activities accordingly.[19] This is not to deny that senators and representatives are motivated by a wide variety of immediate goals, but simply that the principal and essential goal of most members of Congress is to achieve re-election. Even those individuals who are genuinely concerned with good public policy must secure further terms in office if they are to continue their work. In such circumstances the nature of congressional recruitment practices will obviously shape the needs, incentives and hence behaviour, of senators and representatives by generating a set of electoral needs which will need to be accommodated.[20] These may range from access to committee assignments which are perceived as likely to promote an individual's chances of re-election to changes in the congressional workload designed to satisfy the demands of constituents. The increased workload of Congress in the late nineteenth century and in the early twentieth century, for example, was not something forced upon its membership, rather, it occurred because individual members, facing a particular electoral environment, chose to enlarge their own agenda and further develop the institution in order to survive.[21]

In addition to shaping the needs and goals of members of Congress, the nature of the electoral arena will also reward certain political skills and experience, thereby determining the *type* of individual gaining election. This factor is very important because the behaviour of members, particularly their attitudes towards authority, is partly shaped by their past experience and current political skills. There is a distinct contrast in legislative style, in fact, between party-initiated members and what might be termed 'self-starters' or those who have gained political office largely without the help of the parties.[22] Party regulars, having worked their way up through the party apparatus, tend to be followers and compromisers, while the normally younger, less experienced self-starters are usually less willing to defer to authority. Moreover, experienced legislators are more likely to understand the complexities of congressional procedures than their more inexperienced counterparts who may well be lacking in the skills necessary for legislative success.

The congressional recruitment process not only generates a distinct set of electoral needs, but also rewards and produces certain political skills and attitudes towards authority. It is when these needs, skills and attitudes cannot be accommodated by the institution that pressure for reform may develop. If the practices and procedures of the institution do not fit the needs of its members those members may either try to adapt to their surroundings or, more importantly, try to reform the institution to meet their requirements. Long-term institutional reform may thus be regarded primarily as a consequence of changes in the electoral environment. In effect, elections act as a transmission belt through which changes in the wider political environment are transmitted to Congress. Changes in the electorate, the public agenda, the role of the political parties and the technology of campaigning, for example, will be reflected in the selection of members of Congress, who in turn will exert pressure upon the institution to adapt to the changed circumstances. The 'internal' and 'external' causes of change identified by Davidson and Oleszek may, in fact, be interpreted as different aspects of the same phenomenon: the adaptation of members to a changed environment.

The Primacy of Party Machines

This interpretation means that the 'institutionalization' of the House of Representatives and the Senate towards the end of the nineteenth century may be viewed as a product of the congressional recruitment practices prevailing at the time. Recruitment during this period was dominated by state and local party 'machines' which controlled nominations for political office. Typical was Tammany Hall in New York which by the 1880s had achieved a near monopoly of control over Democratic nominations throughout the state. Advancement was seen as a reward for service to the machine rather than as a consequence of a large political following. To gain election to Congress, therefore, individuals had to work their way up through the party organization. Senators in the late nineteenth century, for example, came to Washington after a long and systematic apprenticeship in lower political offices.[23] In the 1870s, 62 per cent of the Senate's membership had served at least four years in national office or six years in high state office. By 1890 this figure had risen to 78 per cent, and by the 1900s the chamber was dominated by professional politicians who owed their positions to the party organization.[24]

A similar recruitment pattern to that of the Senate can be found in the House of Representatives during this period, and by the end of the nineteenth century it is clear that Congress was the preserve of 'machine' politicians. This change in the nature of its membership had an important effect on the structure and organization of Congress. The very fact that representatives and senators had to face a number of elections to lower political office before gaining election to Congress meant that they were more likely to accept authority than reject it. In the words of the noted Russian sociologist Moisei Ostrogorski, they were docile instruments who owed their primary allegiance to the machine.[25] It is, in fact, no surprise that it was during this period that the strong leadership of Senators William R. Allison, Nelson W. Aldrich and Arthur P. Gorman in the Senate, and Speakers John Carlisle, Thomas Reed, Charles Crisp and Joseph Cannon in the House, emerged. After all, members of Congress during this period were used to deferring to authority and suppressing their own demands. In other words, the 'institutionalization' of Congress during the second half of the nineteenth century should be viewed as a product of particular recruitment practices which rewarded certain political skills, conditioned attitudes towards authority and generated specific electoral needs.

The Progressive Reforms

The growth of a centralized leadership structure in Congress at the end of the nineteenth century and beginning of the twentieth century was predicated upon the control which the political parties wielded over the congressional recruitment process. In the first two decades of the twentieth century, however, a number of reforms sponsored by the Progressive Movement changed the rules of politics by undermining the influence of the party machines in election campaigns. Seeking to make government organization and processes more democratic, and to eliminate the corruption of political 'bosses', Progressive politicians such as Senator Robert M. La Follette (Republican, Wisconsin) and Representative George Norris (Republican, Nebraska) initiated a number of measures designed to curb the power of organizations like Tammany Hall.[26] First, the selection of civil servants by competitive examination was gradually extended in the first decade of the twentieth century. This development undermined the control which the party machines had commanded over patronage, and hence their control over voters. By controlling civil service posts and generally acting as intermediaries in a rapidly changing world, machines such as Tammany Hall gained a deep loyalty from individuals, particularly from newly arrived immigrants. They then used this loyalty to control the electoral system. As Milton Rakove has noted: 'An effective political party needs five things: offices, jobs, money, workers, and voters. Offices beget jobs and money; jobs and money beget workers; workers beget voters; and voters beget offices.'[27] The leaders of Tammany Hall in the late nineteenth century, for example, controlled an annual payroll of $12 million, and with 12,000 jobs to fill were a bigger employer than Carnegie Steel. Second, the growing use of the direct primary, first used in Wisconsin in 1903, meant that the parties lost their control over who appeared on the ballot paper. The direct primary allows registered voters of each party to choose their party's candidate for the general election in what is, in effect, an *intra*-party ballot. Electoral advancement was thus no longer dependent upon the party organization, but could be achieved by appealing to the voters in the primary election. In the words of William Allen White, the use of the direct primary would ensure that 'the political machine is in a fair way to be reduced to mere political scrap iron by the rise of the people.'[28] This development was enhanced in the Senate with the ratification of the Seventeenth Amendment (1913) which provided for the direct election of senators, and thus further weakened the ability of the political parties to influence the outcome of elections.

By eroding the role of the party in elections the immediate effect of the Progressive reforms was to reduce the authority of the leadership in the House of Representatives and the Senate. The reforms not only weakened the control which the party wielded over the outcome of elections, thereby diminishing the allegiance owed to the party leadership by individual representatives and senators, but the fact that individuals no longer had to serve an apprenticeship in lower political office before gaining election to Congress meant that the type of person gaining election began to change. The new members of Congress were younger and less experienced than their predecessors and, as such, were more willing to challenge authority than the 'professional' politicians they replaced. With different political skills and electoral needs from their predecessors, the new members gradually dismantled the apparatus of leadership established by Allison, Aldrich, Gorman, Carlisle, Reed, Crisp and Cannon.[29] Rule changes enacted in the House in 1910, for example, prohibited the Speaker from naming and serving on the Rules Committee, denied him the right to appoint members to standing committees, and reduced his power to deny recognition to members wishing to speak during a debate or offer motions or amendments. Speaking after Republican insurgents had voted with Democrats to abolish the Speaker's right to appoint members of the Rules

Committee, Cannon displayed resilience in the face of adversity by asserting that he was 'Proud to say that men of Illinois take their politics like a Kentuckian takes his whiskey, straight' before proceeding to state: 'God bless the insurgents, for, as far as I am concerned, only He can bless them.'[30] In place of the old leadership apparatus the new members established an organizational structure which more fully reflected their requirements as legislators needing to satisfy the demands of their constituents. Authority was dispersed, and the party's control over resources and promotion weakened by the adoption of the seniority principle.[31]

THE NATURE OF CHANGE

Changes in the structure and organization of Congress may, therefore, be understood and explained by reference to the nature of the prevailing congressional recruitment process. Any institution which is not flexible enough to adapt to the changing demands of its membership will not survive for long.[32] This point is very important because it provides a means of analysing the contemporary Congress. In particular, it provides an explanation of why there should be a committee or party system in Congress and facilitates an understanding of the dynamic processes which shape the institution's organization and procedures.

Notes

1 James Madison *Federalist* (62) in Alexander Hamilton, James Madison and John Jay *The Federalist Papers* ed. Max Beloff (Oxford, Basil Blackwell, 1987), p. 317. Subsequent citations are to this edition.
2 See ch. 10 for a more detailed examination of the floor procedures of the House of Representatives and the Senate.
3 See Joseph Cooper and David W. Brady 'Toward a Diachronic Analysis of Congress' *American Political Science Review* (December), 1981, p. 988.
4 Roger H. Davidson and Walter J. Oleszek 'Adaptation and Consolidation: Structural Innovation in the US House of Representatives' *Legislative Studies Quarterly* (February), 1976, pp. 37–66.
5 Probably the most important study of the changes which occurred in the House of Representatives during this period is Nelson W. Polsby 'The Institutionalisation of the US House of Representatives' *American Political Science Review* (March), 1968, pp. 144–68. For changes in the Senate see David J. Rothman *Politics and Power: The United States Senate 1869–1901* (Cambridge, Mass., Harvard University Press, 1966).
6 Steven S. Smith and Christopher J. Deering *Committees in Congress* (Washington DC, Congressional Quarterly Press, 1984), p. 13.

7 James Stuart *Three Years in North American* (Edinburgh, Robert Cadell, 1833), p. 42.

8 For further details of the committee system see ch. 9.

9 Randall B. Ripley *Power in the Senate* (New York, St Martin's Press, 1969), p. 27.

10 See Rochelle Jones and Peter Woll *The Private World of Congress* (New York, Free Press, 1979), p. 5.

11 Douglas Price 'Career and Committees in the American Congress: The Problem of Structural Change' in William O. Aydelotte ed. *The History of Parliamentary Behaviour* (Princeton, Princeton University Press, 1977), p. 36.

12 See James Sterling Young *The Washington Community 1800-1828* (New York, Harcourt, 1966).

13 Francis J. Grund *Aristocracy in America* (New York, Harper, 1959, reprint of 1839 edn), p. 229.

14 Aleksandr Borisovich Lahier *A Russian Looks At America* (Chicago, Chicago University Press, 1979), p. 243.

15 Thomas Hamilton *Men and Manners in America* (Edinburgh, William Blackwood, 1843), p. 270.

16 William H. Riker 'The Senate and American Federalism' *American Political Science Review* (June), 1955, p. 462.

17 The most detailed account of the changes in House turnover is Morris P. Fiorina, David W Rohde and Peter Wissel 'Historical Change in House Turnover' in Norman J. Ornstein ed. *Congress in Change* (New York, Praeger, 1975), pp. 24–57. See also Robert G. Brookshire and Dean F. Duncan 'Congressional Career Patterns and Party Systems' *Legislative Studies Quarterly* (February), 1983, pp. 65–78.

18 Samuel Kernell 'Toward Understanding 19th Century Congressional Careers: Ambition, Competition, and Rotation' *American Journal of Political Science* (November), 1977, pp. 669–94.

19 David R. Mayhew *Congress: The Electoral Connection* (New Haven, Yale University Press, 1974); Richard F. Fenno *Congressmen in Committee* (Boston, Little, Brown, 1973); and Morris P. Fiorina *Congress: Keystone of the Washington Establishment* (New Haven, Yale University Press 1977), esp. pp. 39–40.

20 H. Douglas Price 'The Electoral Arena' in David B. Truman ed. *Congress and America's Future* (Englewood Cliffs, Prentice-Hall, 1965), p. 32. See also John F. Bibby and Roger H. Davidson *On Capitol Hill* (New York, Hall, Rinehart and Winston, 1967) p. 18.

21 Peter Swenson 'The Influence of Recruitment on the Structure of Power in the US House, 1870–1940' *Legislative Studies Quarterly* (February), 1982, p. 32.

22 See Thomas E. Mann 'Elections and Change in Congress' in Thomas E. Mann and Norman J. Ornstein eds *The New Congress* (Washington DC, American Enterprise Institute, 1981), p. 38.

23 Rothman *Politics and Power*, p. 111.

24 Ibid. p. 128.

25 Moisei Ostrogorski *Democracy and the Organisation of Political Parties* vol. 2 (London, Macmillan, 1902), pp. 539–46.

26 An interesting study of Tammany Hall is Robert F. Wesser *A Response to Progressivism* (New York, New York University Press, 1986).

27 Milton Rakove *Don't Make No Waves, Don't Back No Losers* (Bloomington, Indiana University Press, 1975), p. 42.

28 William Allen White *The Old Order Changeth* (New York, Macmillan, 1910), p. 53.

29 A good account of the Progressive challenge to the hierarchy in the House of Representatives and the Senate is James Holt *Congressional Insurgents and the Party System 1909–1916* (Cambridge, Mass., Harvard University Press, 1967).

30 Quoted by Richard Bolling *Power in the House* (New York, Capricorn, 1974), p. 80.

31 See Joseph Cooper and David W. Brady 'Institutional Context and Leadership Style: The House from Cannon to Rayburn' *American Political Science Review* (June), 1981, pp. 411–25.

32 See Armen A. Aichian 'Uncertainty, Evolution, and Economic Theory' *Journal of Political Economy* (58:3), 1950, pp. 211–21.

4

Congressional Elections

Elections have long been recognized as a central element of a democracy. Not only do they allow a choice to be made between different candidates and issues, but by forcing office-holders to seek periodic re-election they also provide citizens with a degree of control over government policy. Moreover, upon closer examination it becomes apparent that elections have an impact on the political system which goes far beyond that of legitimizing a set of policies and providing access to political power. By rewarding certain political skills and creating a set of specific electoral needs, elections help shape political behaviour, and thus influence the organization and structure of an institution. A detailed analysis of the institution's contemporary structure must therefore involve an examination of the prevailing electoral environment.

THE ELECTORAL ENVIRONMENT

The Basic Framework

Both the requirement to hold regular elections and the basic framework governing such events are delineated clearly in the Constitution. Each state is represented by two senators, each of whom serves a six-year term. These terms of office are staggered so that one third of the Senate's membership comes up for re-election every two years. Initially, senators were chosen by the state legislatures, but the ratification of the Seventeenth Amendment (1913) provided for their direct election by popular vote. Representatives, on the other hand, have always been elected by popular vote. They serve two-year terms, and all House seats come up for re-election every two years. Unlike the Senate, the apportionment of seats in the House of Representatives is directly proportional to the size of the state's population. Under the terms of the Constitution, each state was apportioned one representative for every 30,000 citizens, with each state having at least one representative. To take population changes into account, the Constitution provides for a national census every ten years, after which the allocation of seats may be adjusted. Thus, as the population of the United States expanded, so new seats were added to the House. In the First Congress there were sixty-five representatives. By the Third Congress (1791–2) the number of representatives had increased to 105, and by the 18th Congress (1821–2) there were 213 representatives. In 1929 the House decided to fix its membership at 435 amid fears that the body was rapidly becoming too large and unwieldy to be efficient.

Reapportionment

The fixing of the House's membership at 435 means that population changes are reflected in the *reapportionment*, rather than the creation, of seats. This means that states enjoying population growth gain seats while those with a declining population lose seats. Following the 1980 census, for example, Florida gained four seats while New York lost five. Current predictions of population growth suggest that by the year 2000 California will have fifty seats, a gain of five, while New York will have twenty-four seats, a loss of ten. The Constitutional requirement that each state has at least one representative means that some districts have considerably more inhabitants than others. South Dakota, reduced to a single House seat in 1980, is the largest single district with just under 700,000 inhabitants. The least populated district is Montana's second district which has fewer than 380,000 inhabitants. Overall, the average House district has over 520,000 inhabitants, making them among the most populous electoral units in the world.

Once House seats have been apportioned the actual drawing of electoral boundaries is the state's responsibility. Prior to 1964 this process often resulted in districts of vastly unequal population as electoral boundaries were drawn up to favour one political party. Within a single state districts might vary in population by as much as 800 per cent. Attempts to involve the courts in this issue before the 1960s had been unsuccessful. Typical was the Supreme Court's decision in *Colegrave v. Green* (1946) that the issue was of a political nature and therefore beyond the Court's competence.[1] In 1962, however, the Court reversed its position when in *Baker v. Carr* (1962) it declared that the federal courts had a right to revise legislative districting under the Fourteenth Amendment's equal protection clause.[2] Two years later in *Wesberry v. Sanders* (1964) the Supreme Court held that House seats must be apportioned as near as possible on the basis of equal population.[3] Subsequent rulings have since confirmed the principle of mathematical equality for congressional districts.[4]

Within the framework created by the Constitution the precise nature of electoral politics will depend upon a number of variables. Particularly relevant are factors such as the composition and partisanship of the electorate, and the role of the political parties in campaigns as selectors of candidates, builders of organizations, conveyors of information, sources of funds and structurers of the vote. During the post-Second-World-War period both of these factors have undergone considerable change in the United States. The electorate has altered and the role of the political parties in campaigns has been seriously challenged. The result has been the evolution of an electoral environment which is extremely volatile.

THE DECLINE IN PARTISANSHIP

The present electoral environment facing members of Congress is extremely volatile. Demographic changes and the emergence of new issues have gradually undermined the traditional party loyalties of the electorate and led to a slow unravelling of the New Deal coalition of white southerners, Blacks, blue-collar workers and other ethnic groups which had been fashioned by the Democratic President Franklin D. Roosevelt in the 1930s. Reforms such as the Twenty-sixth Amendment (1971) which lowered the voting age to eighteen, plus the post-war baby boom which resulted in more young voters and the dramatic expansion of higher education in the United States, have produced a younger, better-educated electorate which is less attached to traditional party ties than the earlier generation. The psychological attachment of voters to the political parties has further been undermined by the emergence of issues such as racial strife, the Vietnam War and crime in the 1960s, and abortion, unemployment and inflation in the 1970s and 1980s, which cut across the well-settled lines of cleavage between the Republicans and the Democrats.[5]

Party Identification

An indication of the extent of this breakdown in the electorate's allegiance to the two main political parties can be seen in the studies of party identification carried out by the University of Michigan (see table 4.1). The most significant feature of these statistics is the rise in the percentage of the electorate identifying themselves as either independent or independent-leaning from 22 per cent in 1952 to 37 per cent in 1984, and the decline in the percentage identifying themselves as strong party identifiers from 35 per cent in 1952 to 25 per cent in 1984. These figures suggest that party labels have become less important in structuring voting behaviour. More

Table 4.1 *Party identification, 1952–1984*

	% Democrat			%	% Republican		
	Strong	Weak	Ind.	Independent	Ind.	Weak	Strong
1952	22	25	10	5	7	14	13
1956	21	23	7	9	8	14	15
1960	21	25	8	8	7	13	14
1964	27	25	9	8	6	13	11
1968	20	25	10	10	9	15	10
1972	15	26	11	13	10	13	10
1976	15	25	12	14	10	14	9
1980	18	23	12	13	10	14	9
1984	15	22	11	12	14	17	10

Note: Percentages have been rounded.
Source: National Election Studies data available through Inter-University Consortium for Political and Social Research, University of Michigan.

recent statistics also show that since 1984 there has been an approximate parity of Democratic and Republican identifiers among the public.[6] With Democrats no longer certain of their majority status, elections have become much more volatile, and results difficult to predict.

Incumbency

A number of studies have shown that as the importance of party labels as a voting cue have declined that of incumbency has increased.[7] Throughout the 1960s and 1970s the re-election rates for incumbent senators and representatives remained high as they used the resources of their offices to reinforce their hold over their constituencies. In particular, they used their travel allowances, staff, district offices and franked mail, to build what have been described as 'personal political franchises'.[8] The high re-election rates for incumbents, particularly in the House, have generally served to reinforce the advantage which the Democrats had held in congressional elections even though their advantage in terms of party identification has declined (table 4.2). In the four decades since the end of the Second World War the Republicans have controlled both chambers of Congress only twice, in the 80th Congress (1947–8) and in the 83rd Congress (1953–4). They controlled the Senate, but not the House, from 1981 to 1986 (table 4.3).

The Republican success in gaining control of the Senate following the

Table 4.2   *Re-election rates for incumbent representatives and senators, 1946–1986*

	% re-elected in House	% re-elected in Senate
1946	82.4	56.7
1948	79.2	60.0
1950	90.5	68.8
1952	91.0	64.6
1954	93.1	75.0
1956	94.6	86.2
1958	89.9	64.3
1960	92.6	96.6
1962	91.5	82.9
1964	86.6	84.8
1966	88.1	87.5
1968	96.8	71.4
1970	94.5	77.4
1972	93.6	74.1
1974	87.7	85.2
1976	95.8	64.0
1978	93.7	60.0
1980	90.7	55.2
1982	90.6	93.3
1984	95.1	89.7
1986	98.0	75.0
1988	98.5	85.2

Source: *Congressional Quarterly Weekly Report*, 15 November 1986, p. 2891.

1980 elections is indicative of the fact that senators have always been in a more unfavourable position than representatives when seeking re-election.[9] First, voters have tended to use different criteria to evaluate senators and representatives. While representatives are usually judged as providers of services to their constituents, senators have tended to be assessed against national and more controversial issues. This is partly a consequence of the greater national prominence enjoyed by the latter, but also reflects differences in the size of the constituencies of senators and representatives. With smaller constituencies, representatives are better able to maintain tight control over their districts, establish their roles as ombudsmen and providers of services, and thus insulate themselves from external political forces, than senators who typically serve large geographical and numerical constituencies.[10] Most senators have simply not been associated with constituency service in the past.[11] Second, Senate races tend to attract better quality challengers than House races. This point is important because

Table 4.3 *Party control of Congress, 1947–1988*

Congress	Senate			House		
	D	R	Other	D	R	Other
80th (1947–8)	45	51	–	188	245	1
81st (1949–50)	54	42	–	263	171	1
82nd (1951–2)	49	47	–	234	199	1
83rd (1953–4)	47	48	1	211	221	1
84th (1955–6)	48	47	1	232	203	–
85th (1957–8)	49	47	–	233	200	–
86th (1959–60)	65	35	–	284	153	–
87th (1961–2)	65	35	–	263	174	–
88th (1963–4)	67	33	–	258	177	–
89th (1965–6)	68	32	–	295	140	–
90th (1967–8)	64	36	–	247	187	–
91st (1969–70)	57	43	–	243	192	–
92nd (1971–2)	54	44	2	254	180	–
93rd (1973–4)	56	42	2	239	192	1
94th (1975–6)	60	37	2	291	144	–
95th (1977–8)	61	38	1	292	143	–
96th (1979–80)	58	41	1	276	157	–
97th (1981–2)	46	53	1	243	192	–
98th (1983–4)	46	54	–	269	166	–
99th (1985–6)	47	53	–	253	182	–
100th (1987–8)	55	45	–	258	177	–
101st (1989–90)	55	45	–	262	173	–

Source: *Congressional Directories.*

several studies have shown that the re-election rates for incumbents are related to the quality and *visibility* of the challenger.[12] Incumbents generally enjoy visibility, the advantage of staff support and a positive reputation, and when the challenger is unrecognized the incumbent will have a distinct electoral advantage. If, on the other hand, the challenger enjoys high visibility he or she will be able to pose a far more serious threat to the incumbent.

The most important factor in enabling a challenger to gain visibility and thus mount an effective campaign is money. In fact, campaign spending is more useful to challengers than incumbents because it provides the former with the means to gain the name recognition they require.[13] It has been shown, for example, that when challengers have defeated incumbents they have usually outspent their opponents by a considerable amount.[14]

Campaign spending enables the challenger to use advanced techniques of electioneering to overcome many of the advantages enjoyed by the incumbent.

An explanation of the decline in the re-election rates for senators in the second half of the 1970s can be found in changes in the electoral environment which have allowed challengers to develop more effective campaigns. With traditional party loyalties and labels declining in significance as determinants of voting behaviour, more of the electorate is 'up for grabs', and, as a result, organization and the mastery of new campaign techniques have assumed a far greater importance in deciding the outcome of elections. To a certain extent, representatives have been able to limit the impact of new technology. In particular, they are more able to control their own press.[15] Senators are not so fortunately placed, and the new technology of campaigning has been used by challengers to break the incumbent's monopoly over the flow of information to the voter.

THE NEW CAMPAIGN TECHNOLOGY

Television

At the centre of the revolution in campaigning over the last two decades is the increasing use of television as a campaign tool in congressional elections. Television is the principle influence acting upon the voter and his or her chief source of campaign information. Not only have candidates become highly skilled in attracting as much television exposure as possible, and developed electoral strategies which use television as the centrepiece of their campaigns, but television has also brought about a change in the type of candidate likely to be successful. More attention is now being paid to a candidate's ability to look impressive and perform well before the camera.[16] In short, television has changed both the nature of campaigning and the type of candidate seeking election. It has been 'the most-important factor in reshaping the American electoral scene in recent years'.[17]

Congress attracts just over 20 per cent of network news, and a substantial proportion of this coverage is essentially campaign news.[18] Being featured on news broadcasts thus provides a candidate with a means of attracting free television exposure, and most campaigns are structured with this aim in mind. Candidates are well aware that television is an entertainment orientated medium which requires action shots, and that the best way to achieve exposure is not to give a detailed speech on a public policy concern but to do something which is colourful and has human interest potential. This has resulted in a proliferation of campaign gimmicks purely designed to gain television exposure. In 1970 Lawton Chiles walked down the Florida peninsula to win a seat in the Senate, and in 1972 Dick Clark used the same technique in Iowa. Since then candidates have swum, parachuted, canoed and organized 'workdays' to attract the attention of the media. The latter technique was used with great success by Steve Symms of Idaho in 1972. After gaining the Republican party's nomination for the House of Representatives he 'disappeared' only to be 'found' several days later working in one of the state's mines.

Being featured on news broadcasts has two main advantages: first, people tend to believe what they see on the news; and second, such exposure is free. Its major disadvantage is that the candidate does not have complete control over the content of the message, and is dependent upon the judgement of a news editor. In order to gain more control over their television exposure candidates have increasingly resorted to buying time for commercial advertising in much the same way that a company might buy advertising space to market its product. First used in 1950 by Republican John Marshall Butler, whose spot announcements in Maryland's US Senate campaign assisted his victory over incumbent Democrat Millard Tydings, the use of television advertising is now a central component of most congressional races.[19] Such advertising, it has been suggested, makes a difference of about 3 to 5 percentage points on the final election outcome.[20]

Early political commercials usually showed the candidate delivering a speech or talking directly to the viewer, but in recent years the emphasis has been on image. Candidates are shown on the beach, at basketball games or on horseback to associate them with youth; against a background of bookcases to portray intelligence; and next to the American flag, Capitol Hill or other national monuments to portray power and patriotism. Whatever their respective merits such commercials attempt to create a *positive* image of the candidate, and may be compared with *negative* advertisements which concentrate on attacking an opponent. Although negative advertising *per se* has a long history in American politics its use in congressional campaigns is on the increase, and it has been estimated that approximately one third of all spot commercials in contemporary campaigns are negative.[21] In 1986, for example, commercials castigated Senator James Broyhill (Republican, North Carolina) as a tax-raiser; while Senator Slade Gorton (Republican, Washington) was accused of weakness for failing to fight off plans to dump nuclear waste in his state; and Republican Linda Chavez ran commercials which all but accused her opponent Representative Barbara Milkulski (Democrat, Maryland) of lesbianism.

Negative advertising has also been used by a number of independent or non-connected Political Action Committees (PACs), particularly those associated with the New Right, to seek the defeat of certain incumbents. Following the Supreme Court's ruling in *Buckley v. Valeo* (1976) that the spending limit of $1,000 per year which Congress had tried to impose on PACs and individuals who sought to advocate a candidate's election without consultation with his or her campaign committee violated the freedom of speech clause of the First Amendment, groups such as the National Conservative Political Action Committee (NCPAC) have financed a number of infamous negative campaigns against liberal senators.[22] Typical of these was the NCPAC commercial against Senator Frank Church (Democrat, Idaho) of 1980 which showed a Republican state legislator standing in front of an empty missile silo to underscore the complaint that 'Senator Church has always opposed a strong defense.'[23] In the elections of 1984 and 1986, however, the groups of the New Right changed tactics in an attempt to protect the liberal majority in the Senate. Instead of targeting liberals for defeat they tended to support incumbents facing re-election.

The NCPAC campaigns are significant in at least two respects. First, negative advertising focuses attention on the voting records of incumbents. This has the effect of emphasizing the importance of constituency politics in election campaigns. Second, they provide an interesting illustration of the extent to which the role of the political parties as conveyors of campaign information has been undermined by television. As television has become increasingly important in congressional campaigns, candidates have tended to turn to media and public relations experts for advice rather than the political parties. For example, fifty-four of the sixty-four candidates for the Senate in 1984 employed media experts and forty-eight employed polling experts.[24] Using computers and other forms of technology these consultants are able to give the candidate detailed advice about the direction of his or her campaign. A similar trend can also be observed in House races although the traditional campaign structure which uses volunteers has remained important.

Fundraising

In addition to a diminution in their role as conveyors of information, the political parties have also lost some of their importance as sources of funds because of dramatic changes in the nature of fundraising. The increased use of television and other forms of high technology in congressional campaigns has led to a steady rise in the cost of campaigning (see table 4.4).

It is important to note that alongside this increase in the cost of campaigning a change in the way funds are raised has taken place as a result of the enactment of the Federal Election Campaign Act of 1971

Table 4.4 *Congressional campaign expenditure, 1974–1986*

	House $	Senate $	Total $
1974	44.05m	28.44m	72.49m
1976	60.04m	38.11m	98.15m
1978	86.13m	64.70m	150.83m
1980	115.22m	74.16m	189.38m
1982	174.92m	114.09m	289.01m
1984	204.23m	170.22m	374.45m
1986	238.96m	211.08m	450.04m

Sources: Michael Malbin and Thomas W. Skladony 'Selected Campaign Finance Data, 1974–1982' in Michael J. Malbin ed. *Money and Politics* (Chatham, Chatham House, 1984), pp. 278, 282; and FEC Press Release, 10 May 1987, p. 1.

(FECA) and its major amendments of 1974, 1976 and 1979. FECA places severe limitations on the size of contributions which can be made to a candidate. An individual is limited to a maximum of $1,000 per election up to a ceiling of $25,000 to all candidates annually. Political Action Committees are limited to $5,000 per candidate per election with no overall spending limit. A PAC can also give up to $5,000 a year to other political committees. An individual may donate up to $20,000 to a national political party, and up to $5,000 to PACs and other political committees, but such gifts are subtracted from the overall $25,000 ceiling. FECA limits direct party contributions to a maximum of $5,000 per candidate per election for House candidates, and $17,500 per candidate per election for Senate candidates.

One result of these restrictions is to render obsolete the traditional money-raising techniques of the political parties and enhance the techniques most suitable for PACs. FECA places a premium on an ability to generate very large numbers of small contributions, and the best method of doing this is the direct-mail solicitation of many thousands of names on computerized lists of persons who have previously made contributions to causes and candidates.[25] With their highly motivated membership and centralized organization PACs were ideally suited to take advantage of the new fundraising environment, and between 1974 and 1986 their number grew from just over 600 to just under 4,000 as they began to play a more prominent role in campaigns.[26] The variety of PACs now ranges from business groups to labour groups to ideological groups of both the left and right. During this period PAC contributions to candidates rose both absolutely and as a proportion of total campaign funds. In 1984 PACs contributed $104.9 million to congressional candidates: an increase of almost 900 per cent on the $12.5 million they donated in 1974.[27] In 1986 PACs contributed $132.2 million to congressional campaigns, and candidates for the House were receiving approximately one third of their funds from PACs compared with a mere 17 per cent in 1974.[28] Over 70 per cent of these funds went to incumbents as PACs tried to ensure the re-election of sympathetic legislators, and there is little doubt that PAC contributions help reinforce the advantages they possess over challengers.[29]

The Candidate-Centred Campaign Organization

To a certain extent, therefore, reforms such as FECA together with the increasing sophistication in the techniques of electioneering have weakened the traditional functions of the parties in campaigns and facilitated the emergence of a corps of professional campaign consultants who offer their services to candidates on a profit-making basis. The use of political consultants is not a new phenomenon in American politics, but their use has reached such a level that candidates are now able to develop what amount to their own political parties.[30] These are candidate-centred organizations established purely to serve the immediate end of an individual's election. By the 1980s, the acquisition of campaign resources, the development of the campaign organization, decisions on campaign strategy and the use of the media were being performed by the candidate, not the party organization.

THE ROLE OF THE PARTIES IN CAMPAIGNS

The evolution of candidate-centred campaign organizations has transformed the role of political parties in campaigns. No longer are they the primary source of campaign information, finance and expertise. Indeed, rather than attempting to structure the vote, both the Democratic and Republican parties now act as support agencies for their candidates. Essentially, the parties now provide candidate-centred services rather than voter-centred services.[32] Both parties realise that in an era of candidate-centred campaigns winning elections requires good candidates. As a result, both attempt to ensure that their candidates are well placed to take advantage of the new technology, and thus wage effective campaigns. In the words of Charles T. Mannat, Chairman of the Democratic National Committee (DNC): 'We want to have the best-informed, best-prepared candidates and campaign managers we possibly can.'[33]

One of the means by which the Republican and Democratic National Committees have tried to provide assistance to their candidates is through the establishment of Campaign Management Colleges. Established in 1974 and 1981 respectively, these Colleges give managers of congressional campaigns sophisticated training in campaign techniques. The national committees also provide candidates with studies of voters, non-voters, campaign managers and polls conducted by national polling firms. In order to help candidates solicit PACs and political consultants the national committees have designed 'PAC-Kits'. These provide candidates with a list of sympathetic PACs and an evaluative catalogue of political consultants.

The Congressional Campaign Committees

Although the services provided by the RNC and DNC are important, of perhaps more significance to candidates running for Congress has been the recent 'institutionalization' of the parties' congressional campaign committees: the Democratic Congressional Campaign Committee (DCCC) and the National Republican Congressional Committee (NRCC) in the House, and the Democratic Senatorial Campaign Committee (DSCC) and the National Republican Senatorial Committee (NRSC) in the Senate. These committees are permanently staffed by full-time professional party workers, and have become important centres of campaign activity.[34] Like the RNC and DNC the congressional campaign committees maintain lists of campaign managers, media consultants, pollsters, direct-mail specialists and other campaign professionals.[35] They also provide candidates with information about campaign techniques. The NRCC, for example, provides Republican candidates with monthly video-cassettes dealing with topics ranging from debating strategy to the Federal budget-reducing law. It also publishes a paper *Incumbent* which it distributes free to candidates. One edition published in 1986 focused on the technique of speech-making. It advised candidates to: 'People-ize, people-ize, people-ize. If it doesn't involve people it's not an issue. Don't say "Because of failed Democratic farm policies, 10,000 farmers will lose their farms" say "Because of failed Democratic policies, Ralph and Edna Johnson of Alta will lose their farm. They're just one of 10,000 families . . ."'[36]

A further indication of the type of support now given to the candidates by the political parties can be seen in the activities of the Republican Conference (caucus) in the Senate. In 1981, the chairman of the Conference, Senator James McClure (Republican, Idaho), hired Carter L. Clews, the former director of public relations for the National Right to Work Committee, as the director of the Conference's communications division, and greatly expanded the media facilities available to senators. A print unit has become responsible for mailing reports on Republican senators to news editors across the United States. Telephone and television requirements are met by an electronics unit which provides a range of services from video recording to radio broadcasting. Finally, a graphic arts unit assists in preparing newsletters and press releases.[37]

In addition to the type of personal campaign assistance provided by the congressional campaign committees and the Republican Conference, the national parties also engage in 'genre' advertising which is designed to improve the general image of the party rather than promote a specific individual. A typical example of this form of advertising was the $9.4 million campaign 'Vote Republican – For A Change' which was run by the RNC in 1980. This campaign was designed to place the blame for the United States's problems on the preceding twenty-five years of Democratic control of Congress. The first commercial, which was shown on 29 January 1980, featured a look-alike of the speaker of the House of Representatives Tip O'Neill driving a large American car until it ran out of petrol while a voice-over declared: 'The Democrats actually passed laws that cut back on energy exploration here at home and made us dependent upon foreign oil.' Other commercials showed a dollar bill shrinking in the hands of a worker to the size of a postage stamp to illustrate the effects of inflation, and another showed a pair of hands counting out money at what was described as the congressional spending rate of 'a million dollars a minute'. Similar campaigns were run by the Republicans in 1982 with their 'Stay the Course' series of commercials, and in 1984 with their 'America's Back Again' slots. The Democrats finally adopted 'genre' advertising in 1982 when the DNC produced a series of commercials called 'It Isn't Fair. It's Republican.'

Co-ordinated Expenditures

The use of 'genre' advertising is, in many respects, a consequence of FECA's limitations on contributions to candidates. Unable to give direct contributions of more than $5,000 to House candidates and $17,500 to Senate candidates, the parties employ other means of providing financial assistance. In addition to paying for 'genre' advertising, the parties also make 'co-ordinated expenditures' on behalf of candidates. Co-ordinated expenditures can be made for almost any campaign activity as long as the party retains some control over how the money is spent. Typically, the national parties pay for opinion polls, campaign advertisements and media time: all major expenses in areas where some expertise is required.[38] Unlike the limits on direct contributions, co-ordinated spending limits are adjusted for inflation. The limit for House campaigns is currently just over $20,000, while the

Table 4.5 *Party contributions and expenditures on behalf of
candidates as a percentage of total funding, 1976–1986*

	Senate	House
1976		
Democrat	2	4
Republican	6	13
1978		
Democrat	3	3
Republican	8	11
1980		
Democrat	4	2
Republican	15	9
1982		
Democrat	4	2
Republican	16	10
1984		
Democrat	4	2
Republican	8	11
1986		
Democrat	4	2
Republican	11	6

Note: Percentages have been rounded.
Sources: Michael J. Malbin and Thomas W. Skladony 'Selected
Campaign Finance Data', pp. 288–9; FEC Reports on Financial
Activity 1983–1984, *Final Report*, 'US Senate and House Cam-
paigns' (November), 1985, p. 5; and FEC Press Release, 10 May
1987, p. 6.

limit for Senate races is two cents multiplied by the state's voting age
population, adjusted for inflation since 1974.

By making co-ordinated expenditures on behalf of candidates the
Republican party, in particular, is now a useful source of funds for
candidates (table 4.5). The ability of the national parties to give financial
aid, and offer services to their candidates is, of course, dependent upon
their ability to raise funds. In this respect, the Republican advantage
detailed in table 4.5 merely reflects the party's success in raising funds. All
three Republican National Committees run very successful direct-mail
operations, and despite attempts to modernize their own fundraising
techniques the Democrats are unable to match their opponents. In the

period 1985–6, for example, the three Democratic committees managed to raise a total of $61.8 million and the Republicans a total of $252.4 million.[39] The Republican advantage in fundraising is reflected in the quality of assistance which the party is able to give to its candidates. This point is illustrated by the fact that in 1984 the Republicans held nine week-long training sessions for campaign managers and the Democrats only two. In 1985 the RNC, NRSC and NRCC spent $8 million on outside polling and consulting whereas the DNC, the DSCC and the DCCC spent only $800,000.[40]

A New Role for the Parties

Some observers have suggested that as a result of these developments congressional campaigns have become increasingly centralized, and the national parties increasingly powerful.[41] While there is an element of truth in such observations there is no evidence to suggest that strong, direct links between national political forces and individual voting decisions have been reforged. The use of the direct primary means that the parties have little control over the single most important aspect of campaigning: the selection of the candidate. Moreover, assistance is generally given to candidates regardless of their issue positions. In fact, the parties tend to act as service organizations, or 'super-PACS', whose assistance is useful, though not essential, to the success of a candidate. This point is important because the type of individual likely to be successful in such an environment differs markedly from the type likely to be successful in a system where strong, centralized parties operate. It also means that campaign politics are likely to be dominated by constituency issues because of the absence of a national party platform. Both of these factors, membership changes and the primacy of local concerns, have major implications for the structure and organization of Congress.

Notes

1 *Colgrave v. Green* 328 US 549 (1946).
2 *Baker v. Carr* 369 US 186 (1962).
3 *Wesberry v. Sanders* 376 US 1 (1964).
4 *Karcher v. Daggett* 462 US 725 (1983).
5 For an examination of these issues see James L. Sundquist *Dynamics of the Party System* (Washington DC, Brookings, 1983), ch. 17.
6 See Thomas E. Cavanagh and James L. Sundquist 'The New Two-Party System' in John E. Chubb and Paul E. Peterson eds *The New Direction in American Politics* (Washington DC, Brookings, 1985), pp. 33–68.
7 See, for example, Peter S. Tuchel and Felipe Tejera 'Changing Patterns in American Voting Behaviour, 1914–1980' *Public Opinion Quarterly* (Summer),

1983, pp. 230–47; Candice Nelson 'The Effects of Incumbency on Voting in Congressional Elections 1964–1974' *Political Science Quarterly* (Winter), 1978, pp. 665–78; and Warren Lee Kostroski 'Party and Incumbency in Postwar Senate Elections: Trends, Patterns, and Models' *American Political Science Review* (December), 1973, pp. 1213–34.

8 Gary C. Jacobson 'The Marginals Never Vanished: Incumbency and Competition in Elections to the House of Representatives, 1952–1982' *American Journal of Political Science* (February), 1987, pp. 126–41.

9 See Alan I. Abramovitz 'A Comparison of Voting for US Senators and Representatives in 1978' *American Political Science Review* (September), 1980, pp. 633–40.

10 The ability of representatives to insulate themselves from national economic issues is examined by James H. Kulinski and Daniel M. West 'Economic Expectations and Voting Behaviour in US House and Senate Elections' *American Political Science Review* (June), 1981, pp. 436–47; and John R. Hibbing and John R. Alford 'Economic Conditions and the Forgotten Side of Congress: A Foray Into US Senate Elections' *British Journal of Political Science* (October), 1982, pp. 505–12.

11 See Eric M. Uslaner 'The Case of the Vanishing Liberal Senators: The House Did It' *British Journal of Political Science* (January), 1981, p. 107.

12 See, for example, Barbara Hinckley 'House Reelections and Senate Defeats: The Role of the Challenger' *British Journal of Political Science* (October), 1980, pp. 441–60; and Thomas Mann and Raymond E. Wolfinger 'Candidates and Parties in Congressional Elections' *American Political Science Review* (September), 1980, pp. 622–6. The interesting question of why some senators attract stronger challengers than others is examined in Kenny J. Whitby and Timothy Bledsoe 'The Impact of Policy Voting on the Electoral Fortunes of Senate Incumbents' *Western Political Quarterly* (December), 1986, pp. 690–700.

13 See Gary C. Jacobson 'The effect of Campaign Spending in Congressional Elections' *American Political Science Review* (June), 1978, p. 482.

14 See, for example, Norman J. Ornstein, Thomas E. Mann, Michael J. Malbin and John F. Bibby eds *Vital Statistics on Congress 1982* (Washington DC, American Enterprise Institute, 1982), pp. 64–5, 67–8.

15 See Michael J. Robinson 'Three Faces of Congressional Media' in Thomas E. Mann and Norman J. Ornstein eds *The New Congress* (Washington DC, American Enterprise Institute, 1981), p. 90.

16 See Doris A. Graber *Mass Media and American Politics* (Washington DC, Congressional Quarterly Press, 1980), p. 161.

17 Martin P. Wattenberg 'From Parties to Candidates: Examining the role of the Media' *Public Opinion Quarterly* (Summer), 1982, p. 216.

18 See Michael J. Robinson and Kevin R. Appel 'Network News Coverage of Congress' *Political Science Quarterly* (Fall), 1979, p. 409.

19 See, for example, Andrew P. McNitt 'Congressional Campaign Style in Illinois and Michigan' *Legislative Studies Quarterly* (May), 1985, pp. 270–1.

20 See Charles Atkins and Gary Heald 'Effects of Political Advertising' *Public*

Opinion Quarterly (Summer), 1976, pp. 216–18.
21 See Larry J. Sabato *The Rise of Political Consultants* (New York, Basic Books, 1981), p. 166.
22 *Buckley v. Valeo* 424 US 1 (1976).
23 For further details of the NCPAC campaigns against liberal senators in the 1978 and 1980 elections see Christopher J. Bailey *The Republican Party in the US Senate 1974–1984* (Manchester, Manchester University Press, 1988), pp. 36–9.
24 *New York Times*, 19 October 1984, p. A24.
25 See Austin Ranney 'The Political Parties: Reform and Decline' in Anthony King ed. *The New American Political System* (Washington DC, American Enterprise Institute, 1980), p. 243.
26 FEC *Record*, March 1986, p. 6.
27 See Michael J. Malbin and Thomas W. Skladony 'Selected Campaign Finance Data, 1974–1982' in Michael J. Malbin ed. *Money and Politics in the United States* (Chatham, Chatham House, 1984), p. 296; and *Congressional Quarterly Weekly Report*, 8 June 1985, p. 1115.
28 *Congressional Quarterly Weekly Report*, 16 May 1986, p. 991.
29 For a discussion of PAC contribution patterns see Theodore J. Eismeier and Philip H. Pollock 'Strategy and Choice in Congressional Elections: The Role of the Political Action Committee' *American Journal of Political Science* (February), 1986, pp. 197–213.
30 The most impressive of these candidate-centred organizations is the Congressional Club: an organization created by Senator Jesse Helms (Republican, North Carolina). In 1984 it raised $15 million to support Helms's re-election bid.
31 Robert Agranoff 'The New Style of Campaigning: The Decline of Party and the Rise of Candidate-Centered Technology' in Jeff Fishel ed. *Parties and Elections in an Anti-Party Age* (Bloomington, Indiana University Press, 1978), p. 230.
32 See Edie N. Goldenberg and Michael W. Traugott *Campaigning for Congress* (Washington DC, Congressional Quarterly Press, 1984), p. 74.
33 *Congressional Quarterly Weekly Report*, 5 May 1984, p. 1036.
34 See Paul Herrnson 'Do Parties Make a Difference?: The Role of Party Organisations in Congressional Elections' *Journal of Politics* (August), 1986, p. 592.
35 Ibid.
36 *New York Times*, 26 August 1986, p. A14.
37 A case study of the activities of the Republican Conference is contained in Ronald D. Berkman and Laura W. Kitch *Politics in the Media Age* (New York, McGraw-Hill, 1986), pp. 241–7.
38 Gary C. Jacobson 'Money in the 1980 and 1982 Congressional Elections' in Malbin ed. *Money and Politics*, p. 46.
39 FEC Press Release, 31 May 1987.
40 *New York Times*, 3 May 1986, p. A9.
41 See A. James Reichley 'The Rise of National Parties' in John E. Chubb and Paul E. Peterson eds *The New Direction in American Politics*, pp. 175–200; and Xandra Kayden and Edie Mahe *The Party Goes On* (New York, Basic Books, 1985).

5

Congressional Membership

The stability and nature of Congress's membership has a major effect on the structure and procedures of the institution. While the rate of turnover helps determine the overall level of stability within Congress, changes in the type of individual gaining election may lead to a transformation of both the institution's policy agenda and its rules and procedures. Large numbers of new legislators, immediately affected by changes in the electoral environment, tend to be more willing to provide support for new policy directions than do more senior members of Congress.[1] The elections of 1932, 1958 and 1980, for example, caused significant changes in the nature of Congress's legislative programme, and the influx of new members during the 1960s and 1970s led to important procedural changes in both the House of Representatives and the Senate.[2] In other words, membership changes may not only generate changes in policy but also affect the manner in which the institution's rules are applied, or even give rise to demands for those rules to be changed.

MEMBERSHIP STABILITY

Voluntary Retirements

The generally high re-election rates for incumbent representatives and senators give a misleading impression of membership stability in Congress over the last twenty-five years. By focusing on the success or failure of incumbents seeking re-election they fail to take account of either those who die in office, or those who simply do not stand for re-election. While the number of members who die in office has remained fairly constant, the number who retire voluntarily from the House and Senate, either for personal reasons or to seek election to another office, has fluctuated

Table 5.1   *Voluntary retirements from Congress, 1962–1986*

	House	Senate
1962	24	4
1964	33	2
1966	22	3
1968	23	6
1970	29	4
1972	40	6
1974	43	7
1976	47	8
1978	49	10
1980	34	5
1982	39	3
1984	22	4
1986	39	6

Source: Compiled from data given in the *Congressional Quarterly Weekly Report*, 1962–86.

considerably (table 5.1). The number of voluntary retirements from both the House and the Senate rose steadily throughout the 1970s, reaching a peak in 1978. In that year 10 per cent of the Senate and 11 per cent of the House retired. Since then the number of retirements has fallen slightly, though the number of representatives not seeking re-election is still higher than in the 1960s.

What is interesting about these figures is the fact that voluntary retirement has become the largest source of turnover in the House. With the sole exception of 1980 the number of retirements has exceeded the number of defeats in elections since 1970; just the opposite of the pattern that existed between 1946 and the mid-1960s. The reasons for the increase in retirements are diverse. In many respects the job of the representative is much harder: the life is more unpleasant, the workload is overwhelming and the financial incentives to retire are greater, particularly as pensions have been increased while congressional salaries have generally failed to keep pace with inflation.[3] Quite simply, the job has become less attractive.[4] By contrast, despite an increase in the number of voluntary retirements during the 1970s, the main source of turnover in the Senate has remained electoral defeat.

Voluntary retirements clearly need to be taken into account when calculating membership stability in Congress. One means of doing this is to determine the total number of freshmen entering Congress at each

Table 5.2 *The number of freshmen entering Congress, 1962–1986*

	House	Senate
1962	66	12
1964	83	8
1966	60	7
1968	36	15
1970	48	11
1972	67	13
1974	86	11
1976	64	18
1978	77	20
1980	73	18
1982	80	5
1984	43	7
1986	50	13

Sources: Norman J. Ornstein, Thomas E. Mann, Michael J. Malbin, John F. Bibby *Vital Statistics on Congress 1982* (Washington DC, American Enterprise Institute, 1982), pp. 16–17; and *Congressional Quarterly Weekly Report*, 8 November 1986, p. 2815.

election (table 5.2). The proportion of freshmen representatives reached a low point of 8 per cent in 1968, only to rise in the seven subsequent elections before declining in the mid-1980s. A similar pattern can be observed in the Senate with the proportion of freshmen gaining election rising throughout the 1970s only to fall dramatically in the early 1980s.

The Importance of Membership Turnover

The level of membership turnover is, in fact, very important. A degree of stability, for example, is essential for the functioning of the seniority system. Only in a fairly stable environment, with a low level of turnover, is it likely that freshmen will be willing to wait their turn to assume the advantages of seniority. With a high rate of turnover, the much larger cadre of junior members might well begin to reassess the wisdom of waiting to enjoy the benefits of long service, and consequently might call for changes in the rules. In this sense the relative stability of the membership of the House during the 1960s reinforced the existing rules and procedures. It was only with the large influx of freshmen following the 1972 and 1974 elections that sufficient pressure emerged to challenge these rules. In the Senate this process began a little earlier, following the Democratic landslide of 1958, and continued throughout the 1960s and 1970s. By the 1980s, however, the re-establishment of a more stable membership level contributed to a decline in the pressure for further procedural reforms in both chambers.

Institutional change is also linked to turnover rates in another, slightly more subtle, manner. Every institution has written and unwritten rules. The latter, commonly called norms or folkways, are the informal 'rules of the game' which govern behaviour in an institution like the US Congress. Studies conducted in the 1960s identified similar norms in both the House and the Senate.[5] Typical were the six norms cited by Donald R. Matthews in what was probably the most influential of these studies. Matthews found that the Senate demanded a certain style and character from its members that could only be acquired by serving a period of *apprenticeship* in which junior senators were expected to exercise restraint in debate, perform many of the less attractive tasks in the Senate and respect their seniors.[6] Senators were also expected to be *legislators* above all else, and were expected to *specialize* in one particular legislative area.[7] To enable the Senate to function as smoothly as possible senators were expected to conduct themselves in a *courteous* manner and, wherever possible, to help their fellow members in a spirit of *reciprocity*.[8] It is interesting to note, for example, that it was the norm of courtesy which Senator Joseph R. McCarthy (Republican, Wisconsin) was deemed to have broken on 14 January 1955 when he questioned the motives of some of the senators who had voted to end an investigation of communists in government. Senator Russell Long (Democrat, Louisiana), who was presiding over the chamber, called McCarthy to order, stating that: 'The statement of the junior senator from Wisconsin was that some senators were insincere. In making that statement, the senator from Wisconsin spoke contrary to the rules of the Senate.'[9] The Resolution censuring Senator McCarthy condemned him for acting contrary to senatorial ethics, bringing the Senate into dishonour and disrepute and impairing its dignity. Finally, senators were expected to develop an institutional *patriotism* and uphold the rules of the chamber.[10] Only in the House's additional emphasis on committee work rather than floor activity did the two chambers differ in any real respect.

All institutions develop procedures aimed at minimizing conflict. The development of the norm of courtesy, for example, was a reaction to the often violent conflicts which occasionally marred floor debate in the eighteenth and nineteenth centuries. In 1798 Representative Matthew Lyon (Anti-Federalist, Vermont) spat in the face of his opponent Representative Roger Griswold (Federalist, Connecticut) before hitting him with the tongs from the House fireplace. In 1839 Representative William Graves (Whig,

Kentucky) killed Representative Jonathon Cilley (Democrat, Maine) in a duel, and in 1856 Representative Preston Brooks (Democrat, South Carolina) beat Senator Charles Sumner (Republican, Massachusetts) unconscious with his cane.[11] To try to ensure some discipline in debate, members who may be bitterly opposed to each other refer to each other in terms such as 'My distinguished colleague', and personal abuse is not permissible.

While norms of courtesy may be common to most institutions, both the more specialized norms and the written rules of each chamber do need to be learned, and this requires a degree of membership stability.[12] What becomes important, therefore, is not only the number of freshmen entering Congress, but also the ratio of junior to senior legislators. It is from the more senior legislators that the new members learn about the institution. One apocryphal example of this process was related by Senator Joseph S. Clark (Democrat, Pennsylvania) who explained that when he first arrived in the Senate in January 1957, he and five other freshmen Democrats were treated to a luncheon by the then majority leader Senator Lyndon B. Johnson (Democrat, Texas). They found at each place a copy of William White's book *Citadel* which described the inner workings of the Senate. The books were inscribed 'with all best wishes' not only by the author, but also by Johnson who urged the freshmen 'to consider Mr White's book as a sort of *McGaffey's Reader* from which they could learn much about "the greatest deliberative body in the world"'. He also counselled them to 'mold' themselves with the Senate's 'way of life'.[13]

Figures for the House of Representatives show a dramatic increase in the percentage of representatives serving less than three terms during the 1970s and then a slight decline in the percentage in the 1980s (table 5.3). In the 96th Congress (1979–80) junior members constituted approximately half of the House's membership, and the ratio of junior members to senior members, or those who had served more than ten terms, was 3.76 to 1 compared with a ratio of 1.7 to 1 in the 92nd Congress (1971–2). By the 98th Congress (1983–4) this ratio had risen to 5.3 to 1, but had fallen to 3.4 to 1 in the 100th Congress (1987–8).

A similar pattern regarding length of service can be seen in the Senate during this period (table 5.4). In the 97th Congress (1981–2) the proportion of senators in their first term of office was 55 per cent, and the ratio of junior to senior senators, or those who had served over nineteen years, was 3.9 to 1 compared with a ratio of 1.8 to 1 in the 92nd Congress. By the 100th Congress this ratio had fallen to 1.85 to 1.

The relatively large percentage of senior members found in the House during the 1960s was, in part, responsible for the particular set of norms and the collegial nature of that institution during this period. This was

Table 5.3   *Terms of service in the House of Representatives, 1963–1987*

	% of representatives serving				
	1 term	1–3 terms	4–6 terms	7–9 terms	10+ terms
1963	15	41	24	19	17
1965	19	44	22	18	17
1967	14	41	25	16	17
1969	8	37	31	15	18
1971	11	34	29	16	20
1973	16	37	30	16	18
1975	20	44	24	19	14
1977	15	48	21	17	14
1979	18	49	22	16	13
1981	17	47	28	14	11
1983	19	48.5	29	13.5	9
1985	9.5	43	33	14	10
1987	12	37.5	33	18.5	11

Note: Percentages have been rounded.
Sources: Ornstein, Mann, Malbin, Bibby *Vital Statistics on Congress 1982*, pp. 16–17; *Congressional Quarterly Almanac*, 1982–6.

also largely true of the Senate. However, the large influx of junior members in both chambers during the 1970s began to undermine the existing norms. By reducing the number of senior members from whom the junior members could learn about the rules and procedures of their respective chambers, the high turnover rates of the 1970s had an important effect upon the structure of Congress. This point was made by one Senate aide in 1983. He explained: 'We usually changed three or four members at a time. The newcomers were absorbed by the comity, the tradition, the club. But now *they* set the rules of the body.'[15] Without the significant numbers of senior members available to set the tone of the institution it was the junior members who devised the rules of the game. Moreover, changes in the type of individual gaining election to Congress ensured that these rules would be markedly different from the earlier norms.

MEMBERSHIP CHANGES

The US Constitution details only the barest qualifications for membership of Congress. Senators have to be over thirty years old and have been US citizens for nine years while representatives have to be over twenty-five years old and have been US citizens for seven years. Both must reside in

Table 5.4 *Length of service in the Senate, 1963–1987*

	Number of senators serving			
	1–6 years	7–12 years	13–18 years	19+ years
1963	44	27	20	9
1965	29	40	13	18
1967	28	37	17	18
1969	31	37	15	17
1971	27	40	18	15
1973	40	23	19	18
1975	35	27	22	15
1977	43	26	16	15
1979	48	26	10	16
1981	55	19	12	14
1983	43	29	16	12
1985	32	39	17	12
1987	26	44	16	14

Sources: Ornstein, Mann, Malbin, Bibby *Vital Statistics on Congress 1982*, p. 17; *Congressional Quarterly Almanac*, 1982–6.

the state or district they represent, and neither is allowed to hold any other federal office. The only other restriction on membership is found in Section 3 of the Fourteenth Amendment, ratified in 1868, which states that: 'No person shall be a Senator or Representative in Congress ... who, having previously taken an oath ... to support the Constitution of the United States, shall have engaged in insurrection or rebellion against the same, or given aid and comfort to the enemies thereof.' Even these minimal requirements have been relaxed on a few occasions, most notably in the case of Henry Clay, who was five months short of his thirtieth birthday when he arrived in Washington to take his seat in the Senate in 1806. In total, only three senators-elect and seven representatives-elect have been excluded from Congress because of a lack of the requisite constitutional qualifications. On three occasions representatives have also been excluded for other reasons. In 1870 Representative Benjamin F. Whitteman (Republican, South Carolina) was excluded for selling appointments to the US Military Academy; in 1900 Representative Brigham H. Roberts (Democrat, Utah), a Mormon, was excluded for polygamy; and in 1967 Representative Adam C. Powell (Democrat, New York) was excluded for misuse of funds. The latter was eventually reseated after the Supreme Court ruled in *Powell v. McCormack* (1969) that the House had improperly excluded Powell, a duly elected representative who met the constitutional requirements for membership.[16]

Theoretically, therefore, membership of Congress is open to anyone who can meet the constitutional requirements of age, citizenship and residency. In practice, however, Congress's membership has traditionally been restricted to members of certain professions, religious groupings and ethnic backgrounds. Both the House of Representatives and the Senate have tended to be dominated by white, Anglo-Saxon, protestant men who initially trained as lawyers. Studies of the early Congresses, for example, have shown that even during the early 1800s both chambers were dominated by lawyers.[17] Not all observers were impressed by the quality of these legislators. Writing in 1837, Alexis de Tocqueville complained that:

On entering the House of Representatives at Washington, one is struck by the vulgar demeanor of that great assembly. Often there is not a distinguished man in the whole chamber . . . In a country in which education is very general, it is said that the representatives of the people do not always know how to write correctly.[18]

Although standards of literacy improved during the nineteenth century, the basic pattern of recruitment remained the same until the mid-twentieth century.

Over the past twenty-five years this pattern of membership has changed in a number of subtle ways as the institution has adapted to changes in the electoral environment and American society in general. Progress in the area of sexual equality, the post-Kennedy acceptance of Roman Catholics in national politics, the Voting Rights Act of 1965 and the changes in the nature of campaigning have all had an effect on the type of person likely to gain election to Congress. As a result, the contemporary Congress is peopled with fewer lawyers, fewer protestants, more women, more Blacks and more politically inexperienced individuals than twenty-five years ago. Cumulatively, these changes have helped to transform the institution.

Prior Occupations of Members of Congress

Studies of the prior occupations of Congress's membership reveal interesting changes in the background of members of both the House and the Senate (see table 5.5). Although lawyers, businessmen and bankers continue to dominate both chambers of Congress, they do so in different proportions. In the 88th Congress just over 57 per cent of representatives and 66 per cent of senators were lawyers. By the 100th Congress the percentage of representatives who were lawyers had fallen to 42 per cent and the percentage of senators to 62 per cent. These figures suggest that, for the

Table 5.5 *Prior occupations of members of the 88th and 100th Congresses*

	House		Senate	
	88th	100th	88th	100th
Agriculture	45	20	16	5
Business/banking	134	142	23	28
Engineering	3	4	2	1
Medicine	3	3	1	1
Education	36	38	15	12
Law	250	184	66	62
Journalism	33	20	8	8

Note: Since some members have more than one occupation totals may be higher than membership.
Sources: Ornstein, Mann, Malbin, Bibby *Vital Statistics on Congress 1982*, pp. 18, 21; *Congressional Quarterly Weekly Report*, 8 November 1986, p. 2862.

House in particular, avenues other than the law were becoming available for political advancement in the 1980s. In contrast, the dramatic decline in the number of farmers in Congress may be viewed as a consequence of the fall in the proportion of the workforce involved in agricultural work: between 1960 and 1980 the percentage of the American workforce employed in agriculture fell from 6.2 per cent to 3.5 per cent.[19] Increasingly marginalized, agriculture no longer constituted a major recruiting ground for prospective members of Congress.

The predominance of white-collar professionals in Congress reflects the advantages of wealth and education that make it easier for upper-middle-class people to enter politics. Access to the political arena, however, is also dependent upon the existence of other forms of opportunity. In the past some groups have effectively been denied access to political office because of public attitudes and discriminatory electoral practices. Roman Catholics, Jews and women are examples of groups whose national political aspirations have traditionally been limited by popular sentiment, whilst the opportunity for Blacks to gain office prior to the 1960s was severely curtailed by a series of discriminatory electoral laws in the south of the United States. Difficulties in registering to vote, poll taxes and literacy tests served to limit the voting rights of the black population and, therefore, the success of black politicians seeking to represent them.

Table 5.6   *Religious affiliations of members of the 88th and 100th Congresses*

	House		Senate	
	88th	100th	88th	100th
Roman Catholic	87	123	11	19
Jewish	9	29	2	8
Protestant				
Baptist	48	41	12	11
Episcopal	45	40	15	20
Methodist	78	62	23	13
Presbyterian	68	46	11	11
All other	99	94	26	18

Sources: Ornstein, Mann, Malbin, Bibby *Vital Statistics on Congress 1982*, p. 24; *Congressional Quarterly Weekly Report*, 8 November 1986, p. 2862.

Religious Affiliations of Members of Congress

The Constitution is explicit in prohibiting discrimination on the basis of religion. Article VI, Section 3 states that: 'no religious tests shall ever be required as a qualification to any office or public trust under the United States.' Before 1787 many of the state governments had used religious tests to bar Roman Catholics and Jews from public office. Delaware, for example, required state officers to swear an oath expressing belief in the Holy Trinity, while Georgia required that they be of the protestant religion. Despite the provisions of the Constitution, however, protestants dominated American political life until the beginning of the twentieth century. Since then, the influence of protestantism has gradually declined, and the protestant domination of national politics was ended with the election of John F. Kennedy as President in 1960. Between 1963 and 1987 the number of Roman Catholics in Congress almost doubled, and the number of Jews more than tripled. By the 100th Congress Roman Catholics constituted 28 per cent of the membership of the House and 19 per cent of the Senate; 7 per cent of representatives and 8 per cent of senators were Jewish, and the strength of the mainstream protestant groups had declined. In the 88th Congress 55 per cent of representatives and 65 per cent of senators had belonged to the Baptist, Episcopalian, Methodist or Presbyterian churches. These percentages had fallen to 43 per cent and 55 per cent respectively by the 100th Congress (see table 5.6).

Women in Congress

The changes in the religious affiliations of members of Congress reflects the general assimilation of Roman Catholics and Jews into the mainstream of American life. A similar process can also be observed with regard to the role of women in the political arena. American women were guaranteed the right to vote in 1920 with the ratification of the Nineteenth Amendment. Despite this fact it was not until the 1950s and 1960s, when the traditional stereotype of a woman's role in society began to be successfully challenged, that women began to gain election to Congress in their own right. Previously the few women who had served in Congress had tended to be appointed, usually following the death of their husbands in office.[20] Between 1920 and 1950 the number of women in the House of Representatives averaged approximately six in each Congress. By the 100th Congress twenty-three representatives and two senators were women.

Blacks in Congress

As with women and the religious minorities, black Americans have in the past been restricted in their attempts to gain political office by the general attitudes of the majority. Unlike these other groups, however, the opportunities for Blacks were also limited by discriminatory electoral practices. Although the Fifteenth Amendment, ratified in 1870, declared that: 'The right of citizens of the United States to vote shall not be denied or abridged by the United States or by any State on account of race, color, or previous condition of servitude', the black population of the south of the United States was effectively disfranchised until the 1960s through devices such as the poll tax, literacy tests and physical intimidation. Before the passage of the Voting Rights Act (1965) only one in four adult Blacks had managed to register to vote in the states of Alabama, Georgia, Louisiana, Mississippi, North Carolina, South Carolina and Virginia. To rectify this situation the Voting Rights Act suspended literacy tests in any county where less than 50 per cent of the eligible electorate had registered to vote in 1964, and dispatched federal examiners to register prospective voters in any country practising voting discrimination. These provisions were strengthened by the Supreme Court's ruling in *Harper v. Virgina State Board of Elections* (1966) that poll taxes were unconstitutional.[21] By 1982, when the Voting Rights Act was extended for the third time, approximately 60 per cent of black southerners had been registered to vote.[22] At the national level this enfranchisement of the black population resulted in a dramatic increase in the number of black members of Congress. In the 100th Congress there were twenty-three black representatives compared with a mere four in the 88th Congress. Between 1877 and 1960 there had been approximately one black representative in each Congress. The first black senator since federal troops were withdrawn from the south in 1877, Edward Brooke (Republican, Massachusetts), lost his seat in 1978 after being targeted for defeat by various New Right groups.[23]

Generational Changes

The gradual broadening of Congress's *social* base in the past twenty-five years has led to certain changes in policy preferences. The growing number of Roman Catholics, for example, has provided a sizable constituency for anti-abortion legislation, and some commentators have suggested that women have more 'liberal' voting records than men on issues such as defence and the environment.[24] Of perhaps more importance, however, have been changes in the *generational* composition of Congress's membership. An influx of younger, less politically experienced, members has led to significant changes in the structure of the House and the Senate. Under pressure from new members both chambers have altered their rules and procedures.

Generational change is primarily the result of new developments in the electoral environment: the individuals recruited to Congress simply reflect the particular political setting in which they were elected. During the late 1970s the qualities required for electoral success were considerably different from what they had been a decade or so earlier. As the role of the political party in the campaign gave way to the technology of television-centred campaigns built upon the findings of opinion polls and run by media and public relations experts, so more and more congressional candidates were self-starters. They developed their own political organizations with help and finance from the various Political Action Committees, and succeeded with relatively little help from the political parties. In other words, candidates for Congress no longer needed to gain the support of the party to ensure their election. Rather, electoral success was largely dependent upon a candidate's ability to take advantage of the new campaign technology, and speak to the ascendant interests within his or her constituency.

The development of the candidate-centred campaign has had some interesting consequences. Initially it freed prospective candidates for Congress of the need to serve a political apprenticeship. The skills required for electoral success no longer had to be learned by serving in a number of lower political offices, but instead, could be obtained by hiring a campaign consultant. As a result of such developments the number of candidates gaining election to the House and Senate without prior legislative experience rose considerably during the 1970s, reaching a peak in 1981. In that year only ten of the eighteen freshmen senators, and thirty of the

Table 5.7   *The average age of Congress members, 89th to 100th Congresses*

	All members	Senate	House
89th (1965)	51.9	57.7	50.5
90th (1967)	52.1	57.7	50.8
91st (1969)	53.0	56.6	52.2
92nd (1971)	52.7	56.4	51.9
93rd (1973)	52.0	55.3	51.1
94th (1975)	50.9	55.5	49.8
95th (1977)	50.3	54.7	49.3
96th (1979)	50.9	55.5	49.8
97th (1981)	49.2	52.5	48.4
98th (1983)	47.0	53.4	45.5
99th (1985)	50.5	54.2	49.7
100th (1987)	52.5	54.4	50.7

Source: *Congressional Quarterly Weekly Report*, 8 November 1986, p. 2861.

seventy-three freshmen representatives had previously served in either a state or federal legislature.[25] Since then, the number of candidates gaining election without prior legislative experience has declined dramatically as a consequence of the increasing cost of campaigning and the continued importance of name recognition in elections. Candidate-centred campaigns require high quality candidates to attract both finance and votes. This fact has tended to reinforce the need for candidates to have held prior political office, and thus possess a certain amount of visibility. In 1987 only one of the fifteen freshmen senators and twenty of the fifty freshmen representatives had not previously served in a legislature. These figures are comparable to those of thirty years ago.

The developments in electioneering which led to changes in the level of previous legislative experience among candidates also had an effect upon the age at which members gained election. With candidates during the 1970s no longer needing to serve an apprenticeship in a lower political office they were able to gain election to Congress at a much earlier age. The increasing use of television in election campaigns, moreover, placed a premium on those individuals who could use the medium well. This tended to favour 'younger' candidates who were able to portray themselves as fit and dynamic. As a result of both these changes, and the high turnover rates of the late 1970s and early 1980s, the average age of members of Congress fell significantly (see table 5.7). During the mid-1980s, however, the average age level began to rise once more as turnover rates fell, and there was a decline in the number of politically inexperienced candidates gaining election.

It is clear that during the 1970s the membership of Congress gradually became younger and more politically inexperienced, but that by the mid-1980s this trend had disappeared. In these terms the 100th Congress had more in common with the Congresses of the early 1970s than the early 1980s. Such generational changes in age and political experience are important because they help determine political *style*. Members who have worked their way up through the party apparatus, serving in a number of lower political offices, tend to be willing to defer to authority, and are generally willing to seek a compromise to gain the passage of legislation. Self-starters, on the other hand, are usually more issue-orientated, publicity conscious and unwilling to compromise. During the 1970s this unwillingness to compromise was exacerbated by the relative youth of Congress's membership. As one Senate aide stated: 'We've gone from older people to younger people, from more experienced legislative types to less experienced types, from guys who know you don't always get your way to those who are bound and determined to get their way, no matter what. There's a lack of responsibility in governing. They don't think they have to be part of a compromise.'[26] Concurring with this view, John Rhodes, a former Republican floor leader in the House, wrote that:

The average Congressman of yesteryear was congenial, polite and willing to work with his colleagues whenever possible. Most important, his main concern was attending his congressional duties. Today, a large number of Congressmen are cynical, abrasive, frequently uncommunicative and ambitious to an inordinate degree.[27]

Increasingly, members of Congress were less willing to seek common ground with their colleagues, were more independent of the parties and more individualistic.

In addition to rewarding a particular set of political skills, changes in the nature of campaigning during the 1970s and 1980s also generated a new set of electoral needs among office-holders. The increased volatility of the electoral environment and the development of the candidate-centred campaign placed a premium upon the prestige and resources previously associated with senior legislators. As a result there were demands throughout the 1970s for changes in the seniority system, in the structure of the committees, in the acquisition of staff and more generally in the norms governing the role of junior members of Congress. By the 1980s norms stressing collective action had been forgotten as individual rights were emphasized. In this way, the new political skills and electoral needs generated by changes in the electoral environment transformed almost every aspect of Congress's activity: from roll call behaviour to workload patterns to committee structure to floor procedures.

Notes

1 See A. L. Clem 'Do Representatives Increase in Conservatism As They Increase in Seniority?' *Journal of Politics* (February), 1977, pp. 193–200; and K. Robert Keiser and Woodrow Jones 'Congressional Cohorts and Voting Patterns' *American Politics Quarterly* (July), 1982, pp. 375–84.

2 For a discussion of the relationship between election outcomes and public policy see Patricia A. Hurley 'Electoral Change and Policy Consequences' *American Politics Quarterly* (April), 1984, pp. 177–94; and David W. Brady 'Critical Elections, Congressional Politics, and Clusters of Policy Changes' *British Journal of Political Science* (January), 1978, pp. 79–100. The most extensive examination of the relationship between membership change and institutional reform is Michael Foley *The New Senate* (New Haven, Yale University Press, 1980). See also Christopher J. Bailey *The Republican Party in the US Senate 1974–1984* (Manchester, Manchester University Press, 1988).

3 Thomas E. Mann 'Elections and Change in Congress' in Thomas E. Mann and Norman J. Ornstein eds *The New Congress* (Washington DC, American Enterprise Institute, 1981), p. 37.

4 See John R. Hibbing 'Voluntary Retirements from the US House: The Costs of Congressional Service' *Legislative Studies Quarterly* (February), 1982, pp. 57–74; and Stephen E. Frantzich 'Opting Out: Retirement from the House of Representatives, 1966–1974' *American Politics Quarterly* (July), 1978, pp. 251–74.

5 The literature on norms from this period is extensive. For a discussion of Senate norms see Donald R. Matthews *US Senators and their World* (Chapel Hill, University of North Carolina Press, 1960); William S. White *Citadel* (New York, Harper and Row, 1957); and Ralph K. Huitt 'The Morse Committee Assignment Controversy: A Study in Senate Norms' *American Political Science Review* (June), 1957, pp. 313–29. For House norms see Charles L. Clapp *The Congressman* (New York, Doubleday, 1963); Donald G. Tacheron and Morris K. Udall *The Job of a Congressman* (Indianapolis, Bobbs-Merrill, 1966); and Clem Miller *Member of the House* (New York, Charles Scribners, 1962).

6 Matthews pp. 92–4.

7 Ibid. pp. 94–7.

8 Ibid. pp. 97–101.

9 *Congressional Record* 84th Congress, 1st sess. 14 January 1955, p. S373.

10 Matthews pp. 101–2.

11 These examples of congressional fighting are drawn from Warren Weaver *Both Your Houses* (New York, Praegar, 1972), pp. 47–9.

12 See Herbert A. Asher 'The Learning of Legislative Norms' *American Political Science Review* (June), 1973, p. 512.

13 Joseph S. Clark *Congress: The Sapless Branch* (New York, Harper and Row, 1964), p. 5.

14 See Charles S. Bullock 'House Careerists: Changing Patterns of Longevity and Attrition' *American Political Science Review* (December), 1972, pp. 1295–1300.

15 *New York Times*, 21 March 1983, p. B6.

16 *Powell v. McCormack* 395 US 486 (1969).

17 James Sterling Young *The Washington Community 1800–1828* (New York, Columbia University Press, 1966), p. 92.

18 Alexis de Tocqueville *Democracy in America* (New York, Vintage Books, 1945), vol. I, p. 211.

19 William Issel *Social Change in the United States 1945–1983* (London, Macmillan, 1985), p. 56.

20 See Irwin N. Gertzoy 'Changing Patterns of Female Recruitment to the US House of Representatives' *Legislative Studies Quarterly* (August), 1979, pp. 429–46.

21 *Harper v. Virginia State Board of Elections* 383 US 663 (1966).

22 An excellent account of the impact that the Voting Rights Act (1965) had on black enfranchisement is Steven F. Lawson *In Pursuit of Power* (New York, Columbia University Press, 1985).

23 Senator Brooke was challenged by the right-wing Republican state chairman Gordon Nelson in the Republican primary. Although managing to defeat Nelson, Brooke was weakened by this primary challenge, and eventually lost in the general election to Paul Tsongas. For an account of this episode see Alan Crawford *Thunder on the Right* (New York, Pantheon, 1980), pp. 279–80.

24 See Pippa Norris 'Women in Congress: A Policy Difference?' *Politics* (6:1), 1986, pp. 34–40.

25 Statistics on prior political careers computed from details given in the *Congressional Directory* 88th to 100th Congresses.

26 *New York Times*, 26 November 1984, p. A1.

27 John J. Rhodes *The Futile System* (McClean, Va., EPM Publishing, 1976), p. 7.

6

Roll Call Behaviour

When a member of Congress casts a vote he or she is not acting and making decisions in a vacuum but is reacting to the various pressures acting upon him or her. The political parties, constituents, interest groups and the President all have some influence upon legislative voting decisions, and their respective importance helps determine legislative behaviour and legislative output. An examination of the way in which representatives and senators decide to vote is not only essential, therefore, to any discussion of policy-making, but also provides an interesting insight into the much broader institutional context in which decisions are made. In short, roll call behaviour is central to an understanding of Congress, and reflects the individual member's relationship with a number of other actors in the political process.

CONSTITUENCY INFLUENCE

Trustees or Agents?

The relationship between the individual legislator and his or her constituents is absolutely central to Congress's role in the US political system. Not only does it legitimize Congress's role as a legislature and give some substance to the claim of 'government by the people', but pressure from the electorate also helps shape legislative behaviour. Yet despite the obvious importance of the link between the voters and legislators, the Constitution does not mention any requirement for members to respect constituency demands. In the first session of the First Congress an amendment to the Bill of Rights was proposed that would have constitutionally guaranteed the right of the people 'to instruct their representatives'. Although such a principle was enshrined in several state constitutions the opinion of the First Congress was that representatives should act as *trustees* for the whole nation, and not merely as *agents* for their constituents. In effect, members were echoing the view of the English political philosopher Edmund Burke (1729–97), who once told his Bristol constituents that: 'You choose a member indeed; but when you have chosen him, he is not a member of Bristol, but he is a member of *Parliament*.'[1]

The sentiment that legislators should act as trustees rather than agents did not apply to the Senate which, because of the indirect election of senators by the state legislatures, was much more susceptible to instruction. Many state legislatures adopted the principle of instructing the senators they elected, and during the early years of Congress, the latter generally obeyed such instruction. It was only with the passage of the Seventeenth Amendment (1913), which required the direct election of senators, that members of the upper chamber were entirely freed of legislative instructions. The Seventeenth Amendment meant that senators were no longer the representatives of the state legislators but represented the people of their states. Direct elections removed senators from the control of the state legislatures and made them responsive to the demands of the population of the state.

Determining the extent to which representatives and senators are responsive to the demands of their constituents has, in fact, been a subject of considerable debate. It has been suggested in the past, for example, that the importance of constituency considerations in influencing roll call behaviour is limited. Studies carried out during the 1960s and early 1970s revealed that voters generally knew little of their member's voting record, and only rarely offered any kind of guidance on how to cast a particular vote.[2] Mail, it was believed, was of little use to the member in assessing the opinions of constituents because letter writers were viewed as a very biased sample of the constituency. Voting in accordance with the district's wishes is thus difficult because it is not very easy to learn what 'the district' wants.

Increasing Constituency Influence

Although political ignorance amongst the electorate remains high, advances in technology during the 1970s and 1980s, together with more sophisticated techniques for analysing public opinion, have helped to reduce the communications gap between the voter and the congressman.[3] Increasingly, members of Congress use opinion polls and election returns to assess the views of constituents. A detailed breakdown of the latter may indicate which groups supported or opposed a member, and inferences may be drawn to explain the causes of that support or opposition. In this way, members are able to gain a more accurate *perception* of the views of their constituents than had previously been the case.

The need for members of Congress to be aware and responsive to the demands of their constituents has become increasingly important as a consequence both of changes in the electoral environment and an opening of congressional procedures. Rule changes during the 1970s, which were designed to bring 'government into the sunshine' by opening to the public committee and subcommittee hearings and sessions in which the bill is considered in detail (mark-ups), mean that a detailed record of a legislator's activities may be kept by any interest group or Political Action Committee. This record may then be exploited through television advertising or direct-mail either to discredit or credit a member in his or her constituency. In other words, more of a member's activities are open to public scrutiny, and this record is easily brought to the attention of the voters. The result has been an increased attentiveness to constituency opinion by both representatives and senators. Votes are rarely made which might later be used by opponents to show how an incumbent has been acting against the best interests of his or her constituency.

In many respects senators have traditionally been insulated from the intense constituency pressure faced by representatives. The longer terms for senators, together with larger constituencies with their greater heterogeneity of interests which tend to check and balance one another, has in the past facilitated a degree of freedom from constituency pressure.[4] Upon first gaining election senators felt relatively little constituency pressure, and only with the approach of the next election would they turn their attention to the voters.[5] The defeat of a large number of incumbent senators during the late 1970s, however, served to accentuate constituency attentiveness. Many of these defeated senators were perceived to have ignored their home states, and this lesson has not been lost on their successors.[6] Since 1980 senators have paid much more attention to their constituencies, and this concern has been reflected in their voting behaviour. These changes were noted by Senator Dale Bumpers (Democrat, Arkansas) in 1982:

The Founding Fathers gave senators six year terms so they could be statesmen for at least four years and not respond to every whim and caprice. Now a senator in his first year knows any vote could hurt him five years later. So senators behave like House members. They are running constantly.[7]

Senators, like representatives, now vote with at least one eye upon their constituents: well aware that they become vulnerable to electoral defeat when their roll call behaviour deviates too much from the policy preferences of their constituents.[8] To complicate matters, members of Congress must also be aware that the constituency in their primary elections will be different from that in the general election. The primary electorate will be smaller, more homogeneous and more politically committed than the electorate in the general election. Balancing the demands of both groups requires considerable political skill, and usually means that a member is unwilling to become involved in controversial issues.[9]

Constituency opinion is an important determinant of roll call behaviour because of the need for members of Congress to stand for re-election. Quite simply, if a member fails to satisfy his or her constituents he or she will not be re-elected. This basic point conditions the relationship between the individual legislator and the other main actors in the legislative process: the political parties, interest groups and the President. While all may influence roll call behaviour to a certain extent, their authority is ultimately limited by the fact that none can guarantee the re-election of a member. Only the electorate can do that.

PARTY INFLUENCE

Low Levels of Partisanship

In most western democracies any discussion of the factors which influence the voting decisions of legislators begins and ends with an examination of the role of the political parties in the legislative process. This is particularly the case in Britain. For example, even allowing for the fact that party cohesion in the House of Commons declined slightly during the 1970s, the percentage of divisions in which 90 per cent of the Conservative party voted against 90 per cent of the Labour party was still over 94 per cent.[10] Although party unity in Congress is evident on procedural questions of organizing the two chambers, only in the House of Representatives, during the Speakership of Joseph Cannon at the beginning of the twentieth century, have general levels of party cohesion even remotely approached the levels found in the House of Commons. During the 58th Congress (1903–4) the level of party cohesion in the House reached an all time high when 90 per cent of the Republicans voted against 90 per cent of the Democrats on 64.4 per cent of the total number of roll calls.[11] In the first session of the 100th Congress (1987) 90 per cent of the Republicans voted against 90 per cent of the Democrats on only 10 per cent of roll calls in the House and 9 per cent of roll calls in the Senate.[12] Even if party cohesion is redefined to mean those votes where a *majority* of Republicans vote against a *majority* of Democrats, the proportion of roll call votes displaying clear party divisions has rarely risen above 50 per cent in either the House or the Senate.

An explanation for the low levels of partisan voting in Congress can be found in the relative lack of party homogeneity, and an almost complete absence of mechanisms for enforcing party discipline. Unlike most European parties, the Republican and Democratic parties have never been 'ideologically monolithic', rather, they have tended to represent different regions and interest groups.[13] Achieving a consensus which unites the various factions within the parties is thus difficult in itself, and is made even more problematic by the absence of disciplinary devices. Part of the reason why partisan voting in the British House of Commons is so high lies with the sanctions that the party leadership can impose upon an errant member: promotion to a position in the government is wholly dependent upon the leadership, and withdrawal of the party whip from a member will usually mean his or her defeat in any subsequent election. Neither of these sanctions has been available to party leaders in Congress during most of the twentieth century. The use of the direct primary, and the operation of the seniority principle, means that the party leadership has little control over either the electoral process or promotion within Congress. As a result, party discipline has generally been difficult to enforce.

The relatively high levels of party cohesion in Congress during the late nineteenth and early twentieth century may, therefore, be explained by the strong leadership structure existing at that time, and the fact that between 1896 and 1908 the two parties were polarized to an almost unprecedented degree. Not only did the dominance of the political machines ensure the election of senators and representatives who were willing to accept the authority of men like Senator Aldrich and Speaker Cannon, but the constituency bases of the two political parties were both homogenous and recognizably different from one another.[14] Such factors, however, were inherently short-term. By the second decade of the twentieth century the authority of the party leadership in both the House and the Senate had been diminished, and changing patterns of electoral competition had all but destroyed the homogeneity of the congressional parties.

The Conservative Coalition

Nowhere was this breakdown in party homogeneity more obvious than in the Democratic majority fashioned by Franklin D. Roosevelt in 1932. The New Deal coalition contained a number of historically antagonistic groups, including Roman Catholics and Jews, but its main division was between white, conservative southerners and liberal northerners. As early as 1936 southern Democrats were voting with Republicans, in what became known as the 'conservative coalition', on issues such as the economy and President Roosevelt's plans to fill the Supreme Court with his own supporters.[15] The emergence of civil rights as a major issue during the 1940s and 1950s only

Table 6.1 *Appearances of the conservative coalition, 88th to 100th Congresses*

Congress	Votes
88th (1963–4)	16
89th (1965–6)	25
90th (1967–8)	22
91st (1969–70)	24
92nd (1971–2)	29
93rd (1973–4)	24
94th (1975–6)	26
95th (1977–8)	23
96th (1979–80)	19
97th (1981–2)	20
98th (1983–4)	16
99th (1985–6)	15
100th (1st sess.)	8

Note: Table shows the percentage of total roll call votes on which a majority of southern Democrats voted with a majority of Republicans against the position taken by the majority of northern Democrats.
Sources: *Congressional Quarterly Almanac* (various years); *Congressional Quarterly Weekly Report*, 15 November 1986, p. 2908 and 16 January 1988, p. 110.

accentuated the distance between southern and northern Democrats, and by the 1960s the conservative coalition was evident in approximately 25 per cent of all roll call votes in Congress (table 6.1). Interestingly, the number of appearances by the conservative coalition fell following the election of Ronald Reagan as President in 1980. This fall, however, was the result of a loss of cohesion among northern Democrats trying to oppose the conservative tide that was sweeping the country, and did not presage a decline in the power of the conservative coalition. Coalition successes in the early 1980s included reductions in food stamps, curbs on abortion, limiting the use of school busing and general support for President Reagan's economic and·defence policies. In fact, the experience of the early 1980s merely seemed to reinforce the claim that the conservative coalition constituted a 'permanent majority' in Congress.[17]

In many respects the conservative coalition is merely an extreme example of the general lack of homogeneity within the congressional parties, and similar divisions may be observed between the eastern and western wings of the Republican party: between the 'frontier' conservatism of the likes of Senator Barry Goldwater (Republican, Arizona) and the liberalism of Senator Charles Mathias (Republican, Maryland).[17] Conservative Republicans such as Senator Goldwater believed that economic individualism could be ruthlessly applied to American life. In his book *Conscience of a Conservative* (1960) he not only ruled out any more federal welfare programmes, but also advocated a staged withdrawal from all existing domestic programmes except those deemed to be part of the Federal Government's constitutional mandate.[18] In contrast, liberal Republicans such as Senator Mathias were willing to employ government to deal with the social and economic problems which they believed could not adequately be dealt with through private means.

Party Unity

Although evident at least since the New Deal, the intra-party divisions in both parties were accentuated during the late 1960s with the emergence of the candidate-centred campaign and the increased volatility of the electoral environment. Not only were the traditional constituency bases of the parties undermined, with the Republicans becoming competitive in the south and the Democrats in the mid-west, but the new techniques of electioneering heightened the importance of constituency politics. The result was a decline in partisan voting in Congress during the 1960s and 1970s and then, paradoxically, a slight rise in party unity in the mid-1980s (see table 6.2). With an approximate parity of Democratic and Republican identifiers in the electorate by the mid-1980s, and a consequent increase in electoral competitiveness, both parties have become interested in making themselves look good and their opponents look bad. To this end they have appropriated the strategies of advertising, credit-claiming and position-taking to build up support for the party in the electorate. There is little evidence to suggest, however, that this revival in partisanship has seriously counteracted the long-term trend towards the dispersal of power within Congress. Coalition building still takes place on an issue to issue basis, and there has been no attempt to construct unified party positions across a wide range of issues.[19]

Although the political parties may form the strongest *basis* for building a successful legislative coalition, partisanship in Congress is limited by a decentralized leadership structure and the primacy of constituency politics. In short, the political parties are too heterogeneous and their leaders too lacking in institutional power to forge unified party positions except on an issue to issue basis. Partisanship in Congress is low because it is at odds with the political environment in which members operate: with the internal

Table 6.2 *Votes in Congress showing party unity, 88th to 100th Congresses*

Congress	Senate	House
88th (1963–4)	41	52
89th (1965–6)	45	47
90th (1967–8)	33	35
91st (1969–70)	35	29
92nd (1971–2)	39	33
93rd (1973–4)	42	36
94th (1975–6)	43	42
95th (1977–8)	43	38
96th (1979–80)	46	43
97th (1981–2)	45	36
98th (1983–4)	42	52
99th (1985–6)	51	59
100th (1st sess.)	41	64

Note: Table indicates the percentage of all votes on which a majority of voting Democrats opposed a majority of voting Republicans.
Sources: *Congressional Quarterly Almanacs* (various years); *Congressional Quarterly Weekly Report*, 15 November 1986, p. 2902 and 12 January 1988, p. 102.

power system of the House and the Senate and, most importantly, with the relationship of the members with the constituencies they serve.[20]

INTEREST GROUP INFLUENCE

The internal power system of the House of Representatives and the Senate, and the relationship of members to their constituencies, are important not only in explaining the low levels of partisanship in Congress, but also in understanding the influence of interest groups on roll call behaviour. To be successful an interest group needs two prerequisites. First, the group must have access to the political system. Second, the group must be able to bring some pressure to bear upon those in power. The decentralized power structure of Congress, and the primacy of constituency politics, provide groups with just such prerequisites. Indeed, so pervasive do interest groups *appear* that some commentators have argued that Congress is a mere tool of vested interests.[21]

Access to Congress

For most interest groups direct lobbying of Congress usually begins at the committee or subcommittee stage. Not only are these workgroups at the very heart of the legislative process, but the structure of the committee system facilitates interest group access. This point was recognized by Woodrow Wilson in his book *Congressional Government*:

There can be no doubt that the power of the lobbyist consists in great part, if not altogether, in the facility afforded him by the Committee system . . . It would be impracticable to work up his schemes in the broad field of the House, but in membership of a Committee he finds manageable numbers. If he can gain the ear of the Committee . . . he has practically gained the ear of the House itself; if his plans once get footing in a committee report, they may escape criticism altogether, and it will, in any case, be very difficult to dislodge them.[22]

Committees have permanent staffs and a steady membership with whom individual lobbyists can develop a relationship and, perhaps equally significant, often rely upon the information provided by interest groups at hearings and meetings to make an input into the legislative process.[23] With the enactment of 'sunshine' laws in the 1970s which opened committee hearings, mark-ups and conferences to the public, the lobbyist is able to play a role in the drafting of legislation, on occasions even suggesting legislative language and compromise positions. In short, with regular contact and reliable information, interest groups have the opportunity to make themselves indispensable to the work of the committee.[24]

When turning from committee work to influencing floor votes, interest groups are faced with a new set of problems. In particular, they must gain access to legislators with whom they may have had no past dealings, and whose offices may be inundated with similar requests for meetings and promotional literature from other groups. One means of obtaining this access, of ensuring that telephone calls are returned, is to have made past contributions to the legislator's election campaign. While there has been a great deal of debate about whether campaign contributions by Political Action Committees buy the votes of members of Congress, what is more certain is the fact that such donations buy political access.[25] A PAC which has contributed to a candidate's campaign fund can reasonably expect to have its case heard. Whether that legislator will then vote for the PAC's position, however, will depend upon a number of other variables: the wishes of party leaders and the President, the legislator's own legislative and re-election concerns and the demands of his or her constituents.

Interest Group Pressure

The primacy of constituency politics means that an interest group with no links with a legislator's district will stand little chance of influencing roll call behaviour. Quite simply, in the absence of a constituency connection, the interest group will have no negative sanctions to use against an obdurate member of Congress: it cannot plausibly threaten to mobilize opinion against him or her at the next election. For this reason, when petitioning legislators, lobbyists attempt to show how an issue will affect the member's constituency. The success of such an approach, however, will depend in part upon the legislator's own understanding of the wishes of his or her constituency. Recognition of this point has increasingly led interest groups to direct considerable resources towards mobilizing grass-roots support for their position. In this manner, they attempt to persuade constituents to bring pressure on Congress on their behalf.

Mobilizing grass-roots opinion behind an issue is not a new phenomenon in the United States. Techniques such as directing mail at members of Congress have been used throughout the twentieth century to enhance existing public support or create new issues. Indeed, it has been argued that constituency pressure rarely springs spontaneously from the public but is usually generated by interest groups and public relations experts. What is new, though, is the use of computer-based technologies and new means of communications to mobilize opinion. These developments have dramatically increased both the magnitude and sophistication of grass-roots operations in recent years.[26] Using computer-generated mail and television appeals, traditional groups such as the American Bankers' Association, and the newer groups associated with the New Right, have managed to stimulate millions of letters to members of Congress. In 1977, for example, the National Conservative Political Action Committee (NCPAC) claimed that its direct-mail appeals had generated a million letters to Congress opposing a proposal of the Carter Administration which would have allowed unregistered voters to enrol at the polls. In 1983, the American Bankers' Association and the US League of Savings Institutions prompted letters with newspaper advertisements, posters in banks and leaflets in monthly bank statements, to gain the repeal of a law which would have instituted tax withholding on interest and dividend income earned by individuals. The latest technique for mobilizing grass-roots support is a satellite telecommunications system set up by the US Chamber of Commerce. This provides subscribing companies with a private communications channel to Washington which may be used by the Chamber of Commerce to alert companies to forthcoming issues, and by the companies to set up a two-way televised meeting with a member of Congress.[27]

The need for interest groups to mobilize grass-roots opinion is testimony to the difficulties they face in attempting to influence roll call behaviour. Although groups may make a considerable input into the legislative process at the committee and subcommittee level their attempts to influence voting decisions will stand little chance of success unless they are connected in some way with the legislator's constituency. In many respects this fact is also true of the efforts of the greatest lobbyist of them all: the US President. As with the political parties and interest groups, presidential influence in Congress is conditioned by the relationship between the legislator and his or her constituency.

PRESIDENTIAL INFLUENCE

It has long been accepted that since the 1930s the Presidency has become the main source of legislative initiatives in the United States. Even Congress's attempts to reassert its authority in the wake of Vietnam and Watergate have generally been unsuccessful as the decentralized power structure and time-consuming procedures of Congress have simply proved to be inadequate for the making of public policy in an age which requires quick decisions and a national perspective. Yet for all the leadership which the Executive gives to Congress, it is by no means guaranteed that individual members of Congress will support the President's position. Like any other lobbyist the President or his or her staff must seek to *persuade* members of Congress to vote in a particular way. Unlike interest groups, however, the President has no difficulty in gaining access to individual legislators, and because of his or her position within the political system, possesses considerable resources to aid his or her lobbying effort.

Presidential Lobbying

Formal access to Congress is guaranteed to the President by Article II, Section 3 of the Constitution which states that: 'He shall from time to time give to the Congress Information of the State of the Union, and recommend to their Consideration such measures as he shall judge necessary and expedient.' In the two centuries since the framing of the Constitution this function has expanded considerably. As well as his State of the Union message, the President now presents to Congress each year a proposal outlining his or her proposals for the maintenance of full employment, a budget message and many other legislative measures.[28] By the mid-1980s the number of Executive Communications to Congress amounted to nearly half the number of bills and resolutions introduced by members themselves.[29]

In an effort to ensure a friendly reception for their legislative proposals, Presidents since the 1950s have held regular meetings with congressional leaders of both parties. These meetings usually take place in the White House and involve the discussion of future legislation and the progress of current initiatives. Failure to involve congressional leaders in this manner can result in considerable problems for the President. President Carter's failure to involve congressional leaders in early discussion of his 1977 energy proposals, for example, led to their emasculation and delay.[30] President Reagan, on the other hand, went to great lengths to involve congressional leaders in the early discussion of legislation, and was rewarded in 1981 with the passage of his budget proposals.[31]

The low levels of partisanship and the decentralized power structure in Congress, however, mean that a President must reach beyond the congressional leadership and lobby individual legislators if he or she is to stand any chance of gaining the passage of his or her legislative proposals. It is instructive to note that during Ronald Reagan's first 100 days in office he held sixty-nine meetings with members of Congress and met 467 of the total membership of 535. If simple persuasion does not succeed the President may utilize a number of other resources to influence roll call behaviour. He may give the legislator a small gift, perhaps a signed photograph, or arrange receptions at the White House or trips on the presidential jet, *Air Force One*, for congressmen and important constituents. In addition to 'massaging their egos' such favours may be of use to the member of Congress during his or her re-election campaign: emphasizing how influential he or she is in Washington. In the longer term, through his or her control of federal patronage and projects, the President may direct jobs and resources into a constituency as a reward for legislative support. Both techniques make use of the member's desire for re-election, and his or her need to show constituents that he or she is looking after their interests.

To enhance their lobbying efforts, Presidents since Eisenhower have established a congressional liaison office, known as the Office of Congressional Relations (OCR), in the White House to keep an eye on Congress and to lobby on behalf of Administration policies.[32] Under Larry O'Brien, director of the OCR under Presidents Kennedy and Johnson, a framework for presidential-congressional relations was created which, with the exception of the first year of the Carter Administration, has remained basically intact. The White House liaison effort was organized along lines which paralleled the organization of Congress, with individual lobbyists assigned to each of the major blocs and factions in Congress. This system enabled OCR staff to establish close personal ties with individual members over a period of time. A decision during the Carter Administration to organize liaison along issue lines was not a success, precisely because it failed to establish these personal relationships.[33] To further increase the resources available for lobbying O'Brien also urged co-operation with the other actors in the legislative process, in particular, with department and agency liaison staffs and interest groups supportive of the President's position.

Presidential Success

The extent to which the President's liaison effort will be successful is dependent upon the degree of constituency interest in the proposals. Incumbent members have seldom been unsuccessful in their bids for re-election because they did not give a popular President enough support, or gave too much to an unpopular President; it is when they cast their votes in support of presidential initiatives which adversely effect their constituencies that their electoral prospects decline.[34] Such conflict between the *nationalism* of the President's perspective and the *parochialism* of Congress is more likely to occur in domestic matters than foreign affairs, and has led to talk about the existence of 'two presidencies – one domestic and one foreign'.[35] Not only do Presidents possess certain constitutional powers which legitimize their role in foreign affairs, most notably their position as Commander-in-Chief of the Army and Navy, but there is often a lack of constituency influence in this area. Moreover, developments in electioneering during the 1970s served to accentuate the electoral liability for members with too great a concern for foreign policy. In the 1980 election, for example, four of the five members of the Senate's Foreign Relations Committee who were seeking re-election were defeated. Increasingly, members of Congress found that foreign policy concerns were politically expensive, and as a result were generally willing to cede the initiative to the President.[36] Only if their constituencies contained important groups which were likely to be affected by a foreign policy decision was the President's freedom to act liable to be challenged. Any issue which causes a reaction in a member's political base is likely to stimulate his or her attention.[37] Pressure from German and Irish Americans upon their members hindered American support for Britain and France during the First World War and, more recently, pressure from the Jewish lobby has led to the defeat of proposals to sell arms to moderate Arab nations such as Egypt, Jordan and Saudi Arabia. Paradoxically, the revolution in campaign technology which has led to greater reliance upon presidential initiatives in foreign policy has also meant that such initiatives have tended to be subject to greater scrutiny for their domestic implications.

While members of Congress may regard a President as having a legitimate right to conduct most aspects of foreign policy, the opposite is often true with regard to domestic policy. This is because domestic policy is far more likely to impinge upon a member's constituency. In fact, a President's

Table 6.3   *Presidential success rates in Congress,*
1961–1987

Year	President	Success rate %
1961	Kennedy	81.0
1962	Kennedy	85.4
1963	Kennedy	87.1
1964	Johnson	88.0
1965	Johnson	93.0
1966	Johnson	79.0
1967	Johnson	78.8
1968	Johnson	75.0
1969	Nixon	74.0
1970	Nixon	77.0
1971	Nixon	75.0
1972	Nixon	66.0
1973	Nixon	50.6
1974	Nixon	59.6
1974	Ford	58.2
1975	Ford	61.0
1976	Ford	53.8
1977	Carter	75.4
1978	Carter	78.3
1979	Carter	76.8
1980	Carter	75.1
1981	Reagan	82.4
1982	Reagan	72.4
1983	Reagan	67.1
1984	Reagan	65.8
1985	Reagan	59.9
1986	Reagan	56.1
1987	Reagan	43.5

Note: Table shows annual percentage of presidential victories on congressional votes where the President took a clear-cut position.

Sources: *Congressional Quarterly Almanac* (various years); *Congressional Quarterly Weekly Report*, 16 January 1988, p. 95.

ability to influence congressional roll call behaviour on a domestic issue will generally depend upon the individual member's perception of the strength of constituency opinion. Recognizing this, Presidents often attempt to generate public support for their legislative proposals through television and radio appeals. Like interest groups, Presidents aim to mobilize grass-roots support for their measures, and thus indirectly put pressure upon Congress. The ability of Presidents to arouse public opinion and influence roll call behaviour, however, will be determined by the communications skills of the President, the issue involved and the general political environment.[38] A study of presidential success rates in Congress, for example, reveals considerable changes from year to year as a President's political fortunes rise and fall (see table 6.3). Although only a crude measure of the success of the presidential lobbying effort, these figures show how President Nixon's ability to influence roll call behaviour fell as he became embroiled in the Watergate scandal, lend credence to the problems of legitimacy faced by President Ford as an unelected President and reveal a sharp decline in President Reagan's effectiveness after his first year in office as he began to pay less attention to lobbying and became entangled in the Irangate scandal. Reagan's success rate in 1987 was the lowest since accurate records began. The figures also reveal significant differences in the success rates of Democratic and Republican Presidents. These differences are largely explained by the fact that the Democrats have controlled Congress for most of this period.

In the final analysis, the President's ability to influence congressional voting behaviour is shaped by the relationship between the individual legislator and his or her constituents. The increasing primacy of constituency politics in the past decade, however, has not only affected roll call behaviour in Congress. It has also altered the workload of Congress, led to changes in the committee system and the organization of the parties and undermined the authority of the leaderhip.

Notes

1 Louis I. Bredvold and Ralph G. Ross eds *The Philosophy of Edmund Burke* (Ann Arbor, University of Michigan Press, 1960), p. 148.

2 An important discussion of this point of view is Warren E. Miller and Donald E. Stokes 'Constituency Influence in Congress' *American Political Science Review* (March), 1963, pp. 45–56. See also John W. Kingdon *Congressmen's Voting Decisions* (New York, Harper and Row, 1973), pp. 30–1; and Donald R. Matthews and James A. Stimson *Yeas and Nays* (New York, John Wiley, 1975), pp. 26–31.

3 In 1980 approximately 68 per cent of the electorate could not name any congressional candidate in their district during the election campaign: probably

the most basic fact of political relevance to the voter. See W. Russell Neuman *The Paradox of Mass Politics* (Cambridge, Mass., Harvard University Press, 1986), pp. 15–16.

4 Richard C. Elling 'Ideological Change in the US Senate: Time and Electoral Responsiveness' *Legislative Studies Quarterly* (February), 1982, p. 76.

5 See Martin Thomas 'Election Proximity and Senatorial Roll Call Voting' *American Journal of Political Science* (February), 1985, pp. 96–111; and Richard F. Fenno *The United States Senate: A Bicameral Perspective* (Washington DC, American Enterprise Institute, 1982), pp. 29–38.

6 See Timothy E. Cook 'The Electoral Connection in the 99th Congress' *PS* (Winter), 1986, p. 18.

7 *Congressional Quarterly Weekly Report*, 4 September 1982, p. 2177.

8 Kenny J. Whitby and Timothy Bledsoe 'The Impact of Policy Voting on the Electoral Fortunes of Senate Incumbents' *Western Political Quarterly* (December), 1986, p. 691.

9 Richard Fenno has, in fact, identified four distinct constituencies for each legislator: the geographic, the re-election, the primary and the personal. See Richard F. Fenno *Home Style* (Boston, Little, Brown, 1977), pp. 1–30.

10 See Richard Rose 'Still the Era of Party Government' *Parliamentary Affairs* (July), 1983, pp. 282–99.

11 David W. Brady, Joseph Cooper and Patricia A. Hurley 'The Decline of Party in the US House of Representatives' *Legislative Studies Quarterly* (August), 1979, p. 384.

12 *Congressional Quarterly Weekly Report*, 16 January 1988, p. 103.

13 James Reichley *Conservatives in an Age of Change* (Washington DC, Brookings, 1981), p. 22.

14 See David W. Brady and Phillip Althoff 'Party Voting in the US House of Representatives, 1890–1910: Elements of a Responsible Party System' *Journal of Politics* (August), 1974, pp. 753–76. For a more detailed study of party voting during this period see David W. Brady *Congressional Voting in a Partisan Era* (Kansas, University of Kansas Press, 1973).

15 For an excellent study of the early development of the conservative coalition see James T. Patterson *Congressional Conservatism and the New Deal* (Lexington, University of Kentucky Press, 1967).

16 See Mack C. Shelley *The Permanent Majority* (Alabama, University of Alabama Press, 1983).

17 See Christopher J. Bailey *The Republican Party in the US Senate, 1974–1984* (Manchester, Manchester University Press, 1988), ch. 4.

18 Barry Goldwater *Conscience of a Conservative* (Shepardsville, Ky. Victor Publishing, 1960).

19 See Cook 'The Electoral Connection', pp. 20–1.

20 Ralph K. Huitt 'Democratic Party Leadership in the Senate' *American Political Science Review* (June), 1961, p. 334.

21 See, for example, the discussion in Andrew M. Scott and Margaret A. Hunt *Congress and Lobbies* (Chapel Hill, University of North Carolina Press, 1966), ch. 1.

22 Woodrow Wilson *Congressional Government* (Londón, Constable, 1914), pp. 189–90.
23 See Carol S. Greenwold *Group Power* (New York, Praeger, 1977), p. 194.
24 Jeffrey M. Berry *The Interest Group Society* (Boston, Little, Brown, 1984), p. 183.
25 For an example of this debate see M. Margaret Conway 'PACs, the New Politics, and Congressional Campaigns' in Allan J. Cigler and Burdette A. Loomis eds *Interest Group Politics* (Washington DC, Congressional Quarterly Press, 1983) pp. 135–8; W. P. Welch 'Campaign Contributions and Legislative Voting: Milk Money and Dairy Price Supports' *Western Political Quarterly* (35), 1982, pp. 478–95; John R. Wright 'PACs, Contributions and Roll Calls: An Organisational Perspective' *American Political Science Review* (June), 1985, pp. 400–14; and John E. Owens 'The Impact of Campaign Contributions on Legislative Outcomes in Congress: Evidence from a House Committee' *Political Studies* (June), 1986, pp. 285–295.
26 See Burdette A. Loomis 'A New Era: Groups and the Grass Roots' in Cigler and Loomis *Interest Group Politics*, pp. 169–90.
27 Berry *The Interest Group Society*, pp. 154–5.
28 See Walter J. Oleszek *Congressional Procedures and the Policy Process* (Washington DC, Congressional Quarterly Press, 1984), p. 32.
29 Roger H. Davidson and Thomas Kephart *Indicators of House of Representatives Workload and Activity* (Washington DC, CRS, 1985), p. 11; and Roger H. Davidson and Thomas Kephart *Indicators of Senate Activity and Workload* (Washington DC, CRS, 1985), p. 16.
30 See Michael J. Malbin 'Rhetoric and Leadership: A Look Backward at the Carter National Energy Plan' in Anthony King ed. *Both Ends of the Avenue* (Washington DC, American Enterprise Institute, 1983), pp. 212–48.
31 See Allen Shick 'How the Budget was Won and Lost' in Norman J. Ornstein ed. *President and Congress: Assessing Reagan's First Year* (Washington DC, American Enterprise Institute, 1982), pp. 14–43.
32 The best account of the OCR is Nigel Bowles *The White House and Capitol Hill* (Oxford, Clarendon Press, 1987). See also Eric L. Davis 'Congressional Liaison: The People and the Institution' in Anthony King *Both Ends*, pp. 59–95.
33 For an account of the liaison effort during the Carter Administration see Eric L. Davis 'Legislative Liaison in the Carter Administration' *Political Science Quarterly* (Summer), 1979, pp. 287–302.
34 Jon R. Bond and Richard Fleisher 'Presidential Popularity and Congressional Voting: A Re-examination of Public Opinion As A Source of Influence in Congress' *Western Political Quarterly* (June), 1984, p. 304.
35 Aaron Wildavsky 'The Two Presidencies' *Trans-Action* (December), 1966, pp. 7–14.
36 Christoper J. Bailey 'President Reagan, the US Senate, and American Foreign Policy, 1981–1986' *Journal of American Studies* (August), 1987, pp. 170–1.
37 John Rourke *Congress and the Presidency in US Foreign Policymaking* (Boulder, Westview, 1983), p. 239.
38 A good introduction to presidential use of the media is Ronald Berkman and Laura W. Kitch *Politics in the Media Age* (New York, McGraw-Hill, 1986), ch. 7. See also Jeffrey K. Tullis *The Rhetorical Presidency* (Princeton, Princeton University Press, 1987).

7

Patterns of Activity

The Founding Fathers intended that Congress should perform three main functions. First, Congress was expected to be a representative institution where individuals not only maintained close links with their constitutents, but were also available to give advice and seek the redress of any grievance. Second, Congress was expected to be a legislature, able to pass legislation aimed at solving the nation's problems. Third, Congress was expected to act as a check upon the other branches of government: able to oversee their activities and prevent any abuse of power. Upon closer inspection, however, it becomes apparent that Congress's ability to perform all of these three functions successfully is limited. Time constraints place an overall restriction on congressional activity of any sort, and on many occasions the three functions have proved to be mutually contradictory. An attentiveness to constituency opinion, for example, often undermines Congress's legislative function. This point was noted by James Madison in *Federalist* (56):

It is a sound and important principle that the representative ought to be acquainted with the interests and circumstances of his constituents. But this principle can extend no further than to those circumstances and interests to which the authority and care of the representative relate. An ignorance of a variety of minute and particular objects, which do not lie within the compass of legislation, is consistent with every attribute necessary to a due performance of the legislative trust.[1]

In fact, understanding the relative importance attached to each of these three functions provides an illustration of the pressures acting upon Congress, and allows an insight into the much broader political environment in which Congress is situated.

CONSTITUENCY ATTENTIVENESS

Although members of Congress have always provided some form of service to their constituents, the *perception* that a large number of members of Congress, particularly senators, had been defeated in elections during the late 1970s and early 1980s because of a lack of attention to their constituencies has led to a reordering of congressional priorities in the 1980s. Taking notice of what were believed to have been the mistakes of the defeated members, both representatives and senators have increasingly devoted more attention to their constituencies. The use of the franking privilege has grown, more time has been spent in the constituencies, more staff have been devoted to constituency work, the amount of casework carried out has expanded and the number of informal, bipartisan caucuses connected with constituency concerns has increased. Together these developments have contributed to a major change in Congress's workload and structure.

The Franking Privilege

The right to send free mail to constituents, or the franking privilege, is actually older than Congress itself. In 1775 the Continental Congress passed a law which provided its members with mailing privileges to help them keep in touch with their constituents. Indeed, one of the first acts of the 1st Congress (1789–91) was a vote to continue the practice. Even during this period, the frank was regarded as an important electoral asset. One senator, quoted by the German traveller Francis J. Grund in 1837, remarked that: 'a man must give some signs of life, or he will not be re-elected. Most of our speeches are manufactured for home-consumption. We "let fly" at them in the House, then print it, and then send a couple of thousand copies of it to our constituents. Uncle Sam, you know, pays the postage.'[2] Under the terms of a law passed in 1973, however, the use of the frank is limited to correspondence 'in which the Member deals with the addressee as a citizen of the United States or constituent.' Prohibited is mail 'unrelated to official business, activities, and duties of members' and mail 'which specifically solicits political support for the sender or any other person or any political party, or a vote or financial assistance for any candidate for any political office'. Mass mailings, defined as more than 500 pieces of identical mail, are forbidden during the sixty day period before a primary or general election. To enforce these restrictions the House of Representatives established a Commission on Congressional Mailing Standards, composed of three Republicans and three Democrats appointed

Table 7.1 *The volume and cost of franked mail, 1980–1986*

Fiscal year	Cost $	Volume
1980	61.9m	511.3m
1981	53.8m	395.5m
1982	100.0m	771.7m
1983	72.4m	556.8m
1984	110.9m	924.6m
1985	85.7m	638.3m
1986	144.4m	1019.0m

Source: *Congressional Quarterly Weekly Report*, 19 October 1985, p. 2110.

by the Speaker. In the Senate, this task is undertaken by the Select Committee on Ethics.

During the late 1970s and continuing throughout the 1980s the volume of mail sent out by congressional offices under the frank rose dramatically. In 1977 a mere thirty million letters were mailed from Congress. By 1980, 511.3 million items of franked mail were distributed by representatives and senators at a cost of $61.9 million. By 1986 the volume of mail had increased to 1,019 million items, and the cost to the American taxpayer of providing this service had reached $144.4 million (see table 7.1). The volume of mail in 1986 was equivalent to four letters for every man, woman and child in the United States. Of this mail, it has been estimated that approximately 75 per cent are constituency newsletters giving favourable reports of the legislator's activities. Indeed, despite the legal prohibition on the use of the frank for electoral purposes, the volume of mail clearly reflects the two year electoral cycle. Only 4 per cent of this mail were individual letters written in reply to inquiries or requests.

Underpinning this explosion in the volume of mail sent to constituents was a considerable expansion in the computer facilities available to individual members of Congress. In 1970 the House and Senate combined spent a total of $732,000 on the provision of computer facilities. By 1985 the annual spending on computers had risen to $75 million, and only twenty representatives and six senators lacked computers.[3] The prime function of these computers is to keep track of an ever-increasing volume of incoming mail. Generated initially by Watergate and then by the grass-roots lobbying techniques of Political Action Committees, the level of incoming mail has almost quadrupled since 1973. In 1983, 153 million items of mail came into the House compared with a mere 40 million items ten years earlier. In most congressional offices this mail is coded according to factors such as sender, subject and location.[4] The computer is used to formulate a reply by choosing from a selection of pre-written paragraphs stored in its memory. Computers can also be used to generate mass mailings. With computerized lists these mailings can be targeted at different groups or even individualized.

Home Presence

To reinforce the effect of mass mailings, representatives and senators are spending an increasing proportion of their time in their constituencies. In 1970 representatives spent approximately fifteen weeks during the year in their districts.[5] By the mid-1980s this figure had risen to just over twenty-five weeks. In other words, representatives are now spending just under half the year in their constituencies, rather than in Washington DC. A similar trend can be observed in the Senate and has raised real problems for congressional leaders when trying to schedule business.[6] Referring to the difficulties faced by Majority Leader Senator Howard Baker (Republican, Tennessee) in trying to accommodate the wishes of individual senators when scheduling business, Senator Alan Simpson (Republican, Wyoming) declared: 'It's like children lining up in the elementary school classroom asking when they can go to the bathroom. "Howard, I've got to be in Cheyenne tonight" or "I've got a fundraiser in Dubuque. Can you move up the vote?"'[7] In both the House and the Senate the net result has been that business, whenever possible, has tended to get squeezed into three days. This partially explains a decline in the time spent in session in the 1980s. Between the 95th Congress (1977–8) and the 98th Congress (1983–4), for example, the number of hours that the House spent in session fell from 1,898 to 1,703, while the number of hours that the Senate spent in sesssion fell from 2,511 to 1,951.[8]

In an effort to maintain a presence in their constituencies while they themselves are in Washington DC, members of Congress have increasingly directed staff and resources to their local offices.[9] In 1970 representatives placed 1,035 staff in their district offices, and senators had 303 staff in their state offices. By 1983 there were 2,785 district-based staff and 1,132 state-based staff.[10] These staff perform many of the functions previously performed by the political parties, in particular, helping local citizens. The result has been an increase in the amount of casework being undertaken by members of Congress and their staff.[11] Many members of Congress now behave almost like ombudsmen, dealing with requests from constituents to sort out problems with the bureaucracy, giving information about governmental publications or benefits and providing general advice. The provision of such services, it is argued, brings electoral benefits to the member: greater visibility and a favourable rating.[12]

Legislative Service Organizations

One consequence of the increasing concern with constituency politics has been a proliferation of bipartisan informal groups and caucuses in both the House and the Senate. In the 100th Congress (1987–8) there were approximately 100 such groups, known officially as legislative service organizations, compared with a total of four in the 86th Congress (1959–60).[13] These groups provide services ranging from forums for discussion to detailed legislative support, and have flourished precisely because they offer members of Congress a means to display a concern for their constituency.[14] In addition to regional groupings such as the northeast-midwest coalitions in both the House and the Senate, the Congressional Sunbelt Council in the House and the Border Caucus in the Senate, members can also display a concern for their constituents through membership of 'industrial' groups like the Coal Caucuses or Steel Caucuses found in both chambers. Membership of a group such as the Congressional Caucus for Women's Issues might be used to demonstrate an affinity with constituents favouring equal rights for women, while membership of an 'ethnic' caucus like the Congressional Black Caucus or the Congressional Hispanic Caucus might be of use in appealing to ethnic groups within a constituency. Through their activities these groups have assumed an important role in increasing the responsiveness of members to their constituents. The information and leadership they provide help members of Congress to identify problems within their constituencies and articulate issues which might not otherwise have been pursued.[15]

The increasing proportion of time and resources being devoted to the provision of constituency services has helped generate changes in Congress's legislative activity. Not only is less time spent deliberating legislation, but constituency considerations play an ever greater part in such deliberations. Members of Congress frequently attempt to direct public projects, federal aid and jobs to their constituents in what is termed 'pork barrelling'. Legislation is often loaded with special favours to members' home states or districts. In his State of the Union message of 25 January 1988, for example, President Reagan complained that the fiscal 1988 budget contained numerous examples of 'pork', including finance for cranberry, blueberry and crawfish research, which had been slipped into the bill.[16] Although pork barrelling obviously creates problems in an era of budget deficits, the practice has been defended by many members. Representative Douglas H. Bosco (Democrat, California) has argued that: 'I've really always been a defender of pork barrelling because that's what I think the people expect of us.'[17] Together with changes in the public agenda, and in the relationship between the Congress and the Presidency, the emphasis on constituency work has brought about significant changes in Congress's legislative activity.

LEGISLATIVE ACTIVITY

Changes in Output

The legislative output of Congress has varied considerably over time. In the 1st Congress (1789–91) only 144 bills were introduced, of which 118 were passed. Western expansion, the development of interstate and international trade and the problem of slavery during the first half of the nineteenth century served to generate an increase in legislative production. In the 24th Congress (1835–7) 1,055 bills were introduced in Congress and 459 passed. The major change in Congress's legislative activity, however, occurred during the late nineteenth and early twentieth centuries. Industrialization and its attendant problems led to new and increasing demands being placed upon the government in Washington DC. As a consequence of these pressures legislative production expanded dramatically. In the 48th Congress (1883–5) 10,901 bills were introduced and 969 passed. In the 60th Congress (1907–9) 37,981 bills were introduced and 646 passed. Legislative production reached a peak in the 84th Congress (1955–6) when Congress enacted 1,921 new laws and, since then, the number of bills passed has generally ranged from 600 to 1,000 per Congress (table 7.2).

Although the number of bills enacted by Congress has remained fairly static over the past quarter of a century, the average length of each enactment has steadily risen. In the 87th Congress (1961–2) the average length of a bill was 2.4 pages. By the mid-1980s the average enactment occupied approximately ten pages in the statute books. An explanation for this development can, in part, be found in the atmosphere of mistrust and suspicion which pervaded relations between Congress and the Executive in the aftermath of Watergate.[18] Prior to Watergate, Congress had tended to pass short, goal-orientated laws which delegated authority to the federal bureaucracies and agencies to work out the details. After Watergate, Congress began to legislate the details, sceptical as to whether the federal agencies would perform according to expectations. As a result laws grew longer and more complex.

Table 7.2   *Number of public laws enacted, 87th to 99th Congresses*

Congress	Number of bills passed
87th (1961–2)	885
88th (1963–4)	666
89th (1965–6)	810
90th (1967–8)	640
91st (1969–70)	695
92nd (1971–2)	607
93rd (1973–4)	649
94th (1975–6)	588
95th (1977–8)	634
96th (1979–80)	613
97th (1981–2)	473
98th (1983–4)	537
99th (1985–6)	664

Sources: Roger H. Davidson and Thomas Kephart *Indicators of House of Representatives Workload and Activity* (Washington DC, CRS, 1985), p. 63; *Congressional Quarterly Almanac*, 1986, p. 5.

Adding to this trend towards even longer laws were the changes in Congress's budgetary procedures brought about by the Congressional Budget and Impoundment Act of 1974. This act created new budget committees in the House and the Senate, together with the Congressional Budget Office (CBO). It also established a new process for dealing with the budget. Each year the budget committees are required to produce a first budget resolution which recommends overall spending limits. After adopting the resolution, the appropriations and revenue committees in both chambers work out the details of the budget. After these committees have completed their work, the budget committees then have to produce a second budget resolution which takes into account the proposals of the appropriations and revenue committees. This resolution sets binding budgetary limits for Congress. If necessary, discipline can be enforced through a 'reconciliation' process which obliges the appropriations and revenue committees to adjust their proposals.[19] During the 1980s reconciliation has been used at the beginning of the budget process, with the passage of the first budget resolution, rather than at the end. In this way, President

Reagan was able to package hundreds of spending cuts in one bill in 1981, force a single vote on the measure and thus gain their passage. Packaging so many proposals in a single omnibus measure further increases Congress's propensity towards lengthy and complex enactments.

The increasing complexity of legislation led to a concommitant increase in Congress's workload during the 1970s. Generated by the need to sort out the details of legislation, the number of committee hearings soared. In the two years between 1976 and 1978, for example, the number of hearings held in the House of Representatives rose by 21 per cent from 3,248 to 3,937.[20] With more issues to be decided, the number of yea and nay votes in both chambers also increased. At the beginning of the decade, in the 92nd Congress (1971–2), there were 456 such votes in the House, and 955 in the Senate. By the 95th Congress (1977–8) the number of yea and nay votes had risen to 1,035 in the House and 1,151 in the Senate.[21] To accommodate this increase in legislative activity the number of hours that the House and Senate spent in session rose inexorably. In the 92nd Congress the House had spent 1,429 hours and the Senate 2,294 hours in session. By the 95th Congress these figures had risen to 1,898 hours and 2,510 hours respectively.[22]

Increases in Staff

Underpinning this increase in legislative activity during the 1970s was an expansion in the number of congressional staff (table 7.3). Both the desire to assert Congress's authority in the wake of Vietnam and Watergate, and the influx of new members anxious to make a quick impact on policy, led to the House and Senate enacting a number of measures which increased the resources available to them. The Legislative Reorganization Act (1970) increased the number of staff serving each committee from four to six. The House Committee Reform Amendments of 1974 tripled the staff of most standing committees. Senate Resolution 60 (1975) provided senators with three aides to help them with their committee work. Senate Resolution 4 (1977) directed that committee staff should be in proportion to the majority and minority members on Senate standing committees. Other measures passed during this period increased congressional allowances for the hiring of personal staff.

In addition to their personal and committee staffs, members of Congress can also call upon four legislative support agencies for assistance. The Congressional Research Service (CRS), known as the Legislative Reference Service until 1970, was established in 1914. The General Accounting Office (GAO) was created in 1921, the Office of Technology Assessment (OTA) in 1972 and the Congressional Budget Office (CBO) in 1974. These

Table 7.3   *Congressional staff, 1970–1982*

Year	Senate	House	Total
1970	4140	7134	11274
1972	4626	8976	13602
1974	5284	12444	17728
1976	6573	10534	17112
1978	6489	11443	17932
1980	6900	11406	18306
1982	6800	11981	18761

Note: Figures include personal and committee staff.
Sources: US Congress, House Committee on Appropriations, *Legislative Branch Appropriations Bill, 1976* H. Rep. 94–208; Norman J. Ornstein, Thomas Mann, Michael Malbin, Allan Schick, John Bibby *Vital Statistics on Congress, 1984–1985* (Washington DC, American Enterprise Institute, 1984), ch. 5.

agencies provide non-partisan, expert analyses on a wide range of issues, and allow members of Congress to evaluate Executive Branch proposals much more accurately. The CRS provides a comprehensive service to all members of Congress, and by the 1980s dealt with over 400,000 requests for information each year. With a staff of 5,000 the GAO acts both in an auditing capacity and as an evaluator of Executive Branch programmes and policy decisions. Each year it publishes over 1,000 reports. The primary purpose of the OTA is to provide members of Congress with studies of the likely effects of technological changes. It also allows some scientific input into the legislative decision-making process. The CBO was created by the Congressional Budget and Impoundment Act (1974) as a counterpart to the Office of Management and Budget (OMB) and the Council of Economic Advisors (CEA). Its main purpose is to provide members of Congress with information to help them evaluate the President's budget proposals. Together, these four agencies employ approximately 6,300 staff.

On the positive side, the expansion of congressional resources during the 1970s provided members with better information upon which to make decisions. This improvement in the quality of information, however, was achieved at considerable cost. Financially, the increases in staff contributed to an explosion in congressional costs. In 1960 it had cost approximately $129 million to run Congress. By 1987 this figure had risen to $1.8 billion. Increased staff also brought about a change in the individual member's role from that of a person who weighs, debates and deliberates public policy to that of a chief executive officer running a small bureaucracy.[23] To a large extent it is staff who draw up legislation, and discuss that legislation with the staff from other members' offices. Senator Robert Morgan (Democrat, North Carolina) was guilty of only slight exaggeration when he stated that: 'This country is basically run by the legislative staffs of the members of the Senate and the House of Representatives.'[24] Moreover, far from enabling members to gain some control over their expanding workloads, if anything the increased numbers of staff have made the situation worse. Not only have more staff resulted in more information coming into each member's office, but the demands of the electoral environment meant that members of Congress wanted aides who could dream up new bills and amendments bearing their employers' names.[25]

The 1980s

The net result of these developments was that the Congress of the late 1970s was spending more time in session, was voting more frequently and was devoting more attention to the details of legislation than had been the case at the beginning of the decade. This pattern of increasing legislative activity began to change in the 1980s. In the 98th Congress (1983–4), for example, the House spent 1,703 hours and the Senate 1,951 hours in session, a fall of 10.3 per cent and 22.3 per cent respectively on the figures for the 95th Congress. Similarly, the number of yea and nay votes fell by 49.4 per cent to 524 in the House, and by 42 per cent to 673 in the Senate. By 1984, the number of committee hearings held in the House had fallen to 2,387. Other indicators also reveal a decline in legislative activity. In the six years between the 95th Congress and the 98th Congress, the number of bills and resolutions introduced in the Senate fell by 7.2 per cent, while the number introduced in the House fell by 54.5 per cent. Care must be taken in interpreting this latter figure, however, as part of the decline in the introduction of measures in the House was caused by the adoption of House Resolution 86 in 1978 which removed a previous limit on the co-sponsorship of bills. After allowing for this rule change it would seem reasonable to assume a fall in the introduction of bills and resolutions in the House comparable to that in the Senate.

In part, the decline in Congress's legislative activity in the 1980s, particularly the fall in the number of hours spent in session, was a consequence of the increasing amount of time spent by senators and representatives in their constituencies. Equally significant, however, was the Reagan Administration's use of judicial and administrative action to implement policy changes.[26] By exercising strict control over the appointment of bureaucrats and judges the Administration hoped to by-pass congressional opposition to its plans. Bureaucrats and judges were carefully screened to ensure they shared the President's views on deregulation and the need for a reduction in budgets. This technique not only threatened Congress's function as a policy-making body, but also accentuated the institution's oversight role. An increasing amount of time was taken up with screening executive appointments and carrying out investigations into actions taken by the federal bureaucracies and agencies. With only a limited amount of time in each session the increased importance of Congress's oversight function led to a decline in the institution's legislative activity. In other words, the Reagan Administration's by-pass strategy lessened Congress's role as a legislature.

OVERSIGHT

The right of Congress to check the activities of the Executive Branch is recognized in the provisions of the Constitution which give the House of Representatives the 'power of the purse'; the Senate the right to ratify treaties and confirm presidential appointments; and both chambers a role in the removal of executive or judicial officers through the impeachment process. Although the Constitution does not explicitly grant Congress the power to investigate the activities of the Executive, the House of Representatives asserted this right in 1792 when it appointed a committee to investigate a disastrous expedition against the Indians led by Major General St Clair. Despite presidential misgivings and claims of executive privilege this investigatory power has generally been upheld by the Supreme Court as an essential part of the legislative process. Typical was the finding in *McGrain v. Daugherty* (1927) that a legislative body 'cannot legislate wisely or effectively in the absence of information respecting the conditions which the legislation is intended to affect or change'.[27] Some limitations on Congress's investigatory authority were maintained, however, in the case *Watkins v. United States* (1957). Chief Justice Earl Warren wrote: 'No inquiry is an end in itself; it must be related to, and in furtherance of, a legitimate task of the Congress.'[28] From a constitutional viewpoint, investigations are permissible if they can be interpreted as part of the legislative process: encompassing the collection of information, the review of past policies and the protection of Congress's prerogatives.

Congress's Capacity for Oversight

Although the *right* of Congress to initiate investigations into the activities of the Executive Branch has generally been upheld by the Supreme Court, its *ability* to conduct such investigations is restricted by the Constitution. Unlike the British Parliament, for example, Congress has no inherent right to punish for contempt.[29] In the landmark case of *Kilbourn v. Thompson* (1881), the Supreme Court determined that the constitutional right of an individual to life, liberty or property, unless taken by due process of law, imposed a severe limitation on Congress's right to punish for contempt.[30] Generally speaking, Congress must appeal to the courts in order to enforce its subpoena powers.[31] The Fifth Amendment also means that witnesses cannot be compelled to give evidence against themselves, while the Fourth Amendment protects the individual from unreasonable search and seizure. Nor can Congress curtail the First Amendment freedoms of speech, press, religion or political belief and association in pursuit of its investigations.[32] As Justice Harlan, in the case *Barenblatt v. United States* (1958), stated: 'Broad as it is, the power [to investigate] is not . . . without limitations . . . Congress, in common with all branches of the Government, must exercise its powers subject to the limitations placed by the Constitution on governmental action.'[33]

While the size of the federal government remained small, the restrictions on Congress's ability to conduct oversight were fairly unimportant. Oversight was concerned mainly with the exposure of misdemeanors by officials of the Administration. The post-New-Deal expansion of the Executive Branch, however, highlighted the importance of Congress's oversight function; adding weight to Woodrow Wilson's contention that: 'Quite as important as legislation is vigilant oversight of administration.'[34] Reacting to the new circumstances, the Legislative Reorganization Act (1946) charged each standing committee 'to exercise continuous watchfulness of the execution by the administrative agencies concerned of any laws, the subject matter of which is within the jurisdiction of each committee'. The act also assigned wide-ranging investigative responsibility to the House Government Operations Committee and the Senate Governmental Affairs Committee to probe for inefficiency, waste and corruption in the federal government. Subsequent changes, initiated in the wake of Vietnam and Watergate, have extended Congress's authority and resources for oversight. The Intergovernmental Cooperation Act (1968) required committees having jurisdictions over grants-in-aid to conduct studies of these programmes. The Legislative Reorganization Act (1970) directed most committees to issue biennial reports on their oversight responsibilities. The House Committee Reform Amendments of 1974 and Senate Resolution 4 (1977) assigned 'special' or 'comprehensive' oversight responsibilities, similar to those given to the House Government Operations Committee and Senate Governmental Affairs Committee, to several standing committees. The House also provided for the establishment of oversight subcommittees on each committee.

Techniques of Oversight

In addition to strengthening its investigative capacity, Congress also began to make much greater use of the legislative veto during the 1970s to control the Executive.[35] First used in 1932, the legislative veto is a provision within a statute which enables Congress, by majority vote, to veto certain Executive Branch initiatives and regulations. It is, in fact, a central feature of both the War Powers Resolution (1973) and the Congressional Budget and Impoundment Act (1974). Although employed in over 200 statutes, the legislative veto was declared unconstitutional by the Supreme Court in *Immigration and Naturalization Service v. Chadha* (1983).[36] The Court determined that the device violated the separation of powers, the principle of bicameralism and Article I, Section 7 of the Constitution which stated that legislation passed by both chambers of Congress should be presented to the President for his signature or veto. In its way, the implications of this decision were enormous. As Justice Byron White noted in a written dissent issued with the *Chadha* ruling, the decision 'strikes down in one fell swoop provisions in more laws enacted by Congress than the Court has cumulatively invalidated in its entire history'.

Denied the use of one of its favoured techniques of oversight, Congress has been forced to search for others. One method which has increasingly found favour has been an attempt to control the Executive through the appropriations process. In other words, Congress has resorted to using its 'power of the purse'. As well as placing problematic departments and agencies on temporary authorizations which force bureaucrats to appear before Congress each year to justify their actions, the adjustment of levels of funding can also be used to define programmes. By increasing or reducing funding for programmes, Congress can exert an influence over the implementation of public policy. The Reagan Adminstration's technique of appointing administrators who are unsympathetic to the goals of many programmes, however, has also forced Congress to pay far more attention to executive nominations. By the mid-1980s, public hearings were held for approximately two-thirds of all executive nominees compared with a mere half fifteen years earlier. The rejection of Judge Bork, one of President Reagan's nominees for the Supreme Court, also reveals a willingness by the Senate to assert its constitutional prerogatives.

Implicit in Congress's use of temporary authorizations and the legislative veto is a recognition of the changing purpose of oversight. Oversight had traditionally been viewed as involving a retrospective examination of the performance of administrators. Essentially, it was viewed as a 'review after the fact'.[37] More recently, oversight has been understood to mean that Congress should play an active role in the execution of policy. In other words, congressional oversight has moved away from a mere evaluation of past administrative performance, and instead requires a continuous evaluation of present administrative performance. Whether Congress can actually perform such a role is a question which has aroused a great deal of debate.

There can be little doubt that Congress is engaged in more oversight activity. Pressure from the public and the Reagan Administrations's use of by-pass strategies have forced the institution to expand its oversight resources. Members of the Administration have increasingly begun to complain about the number of hearings which they are forced to attend. In 1985, for example, Terrence M. Scanlon, chairman of the Consumer Product Safety Commission, declared that: 'I'm not sure that Hill staffers realize the time that is involved in preparation for Congressional hearings. I've just testified at four hearings in five weeks . . . All of them entail a lot of work.'[38] Each oversight technique, however, has its limitations. Hearings tend to be on an *ad hoc* basis with little follow-up. There is also little co-ordination between the various committees. As the final report of the House Select Committee on Committees of the 93rd Congress noted: 'Review findings and recommendations developed by one committee are seldom shared on a timely basis with another committee, and, if they are made available, then often the findings are transmitted in a form that is difficult for members to use.'[39] The use of temporary authorizations is undermined by the need for fiscal stability. With over 100,000 executive appointments to be confirmed every Congress, sheer numbers mean that many receive only a perfunctory hearing. Above all else, congressional oversight is limited by its dependence upon information supplied by the Executive Branch: the target of its oversight.

The Effectiveness of Oversight

Ascertaining the effectiveness of Congress's oversight is, in fact, very problematic. It is difficult to measure both the quantity and quality of oversight.[40] Whatever its effectiveness, though, the increased attention given to oversight, together with the great emphasis on the provision of constituency services, has led to a decline in Congress's legislative activity. Fewer measures are proposed, less time is available for their consideration, and the primacy of constituency politics means that they are more likely to encounter resistance from members concerned about their local implications.

Notes

1 James Madison *Federalist* (56) in Alexander Hamilton, James Madison and John Jay *The Federalist Papers* ed. Max Beloff (Oxford, Basil Blackwell, 1987), p. 288.

2 Quoted in Francis J. Grund *Aristocracy in America* (New York, Harper, 1959), p. 256.

3 *Congressional Quarterly Weekly Report*, 13 July 1985, pp. 1374–80.

4 See Stephen E. Frantzich 'Computerised Information Technology in the US House of Representatives' *Legislative Studies Quarterly* (May), 1979, p. 262.

5 See Glenn R. Parker 'Sources of Change in Congressional District Attentiveness' *American Journal of Political Science* (February), 1980, pp. 115–24.

6 For details of the increasing proportion of time spent by senators in their constituencies see Glenn R. Parker 'Stylistic Change in the US Senate: 1955–1980' *Journal of Politics* (November), 1985, pp. 1190–1202. Parker reveals that the time spent by senators in their states rose from nine days in the 80th Congress to just over eighty days in the 96th Congress.

7 *Congressional Quarterly Weekly Report*, 16 July 1983, p. 1429.

8 Roger H. Davidson and Thomas Kephart *Indicators of House of Representatives Workload and Activity* (Washington DC, CRS, 1985), p. 65; and Roger H. Davidson and Thomas Kephart *Indicators of Senate Activity and Workload* (Washington DC, CRS, 1985), p. 72.

9 See Steven H. Schiff and Steven S. Smith 'Generational Change and the Allocation of Staff in the US Congress' *Legislative Studies Quarterly* (August), 1983, p. 459.

10 Norman J. Ornstein, Thomas Mann, Michael Malbin, Allan Schick and John Bibby *Vital Statistics on Congress 1984–1985* (Washington DC, American Enterprise Institute, 1984), p. 123.

11 See John R. Johannes *To Serve the People: Congress and Constituency Service* (Lincoln, University of Nebraska Press, 1984).

12 For example, see Morris P. Fiorina *Congress: Keystone of the Washington Establishment* (New Haven, Yale University Press, 1977), p. 45.

13 Susan W. Hammond, Daniel P. Mulhollan, Arthur G. Stevens 'Informal Congressional Caucuses and Agenda Setting' *Western Political Quarterly* (December), 1985, p. 583.

14 Arthur G. Stevens, Daniel P. Mulhollan, and Paul S. Rundquist 'US Congressional Structure and Representation: The Role of Informal Groups' *Legislative Studies Quarterly* (August), 1931, p. 416.

15 Ibid. p. 434.

16 It has been shown that the items to which President Reagan objected added up to $3 billion out of a $1 trillion budget.

17 *Congressional Quarterly Weekly Report*, 24 October 1987, p. 2581.

18 See Allen Schick 'Politics through Law: Congressional Limitations on Executive Discretion' in Anthony King ed. *Both Ends of the Avenue* (Washington DC, American Enterprise Institute, 1983), pp. 168–9.
19 The literature on the congressional budget process is enormous. One of the best treatments of the subject is W.T. Wreler, F.T. Herbert and G.W. Copeland eds *Congressional Budgeting: Politics, Process, and Power* (Baltimore, John Hopkins University Press, 1984). A detailed study of 'reconciliation' is A. Schick *Reconciliation and the Congressional Budget Process* (Washington DC, American Enterprise Institute, 1981).
20 Davidson and Kephart *Indicators of House of Representatives*, p. 32. Detailed statistics for committee hearings are only available since 1976.
21 Ibid. p. 62; Davidson and Kephart *Indicators of Senate*, p. 66.
22 Ibid.
23 See Susan Webb Hammond 'The Operation of Senators' Offices' in US Senate, Commission on the Operation of the Senate, *Senators, Offices, Ethics, and Pressures* 96th Congress, 2nd sess. 1976, p. 4.
24 *Congressional Record* 94th Congress, 2nd sess., 8 September 1976, p. S15432.
25 The best discussion of this topic is Michael Malbin *Unelected Representatives* (New York, Basic Books, 1980).
26 See David McKay 'Rational Presidential Strategies and the Relative Autonomy of the State: By-Pass Strategies'. Paper delivered at the thirteenth American Politics Group Conference, Birkbeck College, London, 3–5 January, 1987.
27 *McGrain v Daugherty* 273 US 135, 175 (1927).
28 *Watkins v. United States* 354 US 178 (1957).
29 The Houses of Parliament are able to deal with those who obstruct their business and to enforce their privileges because they are the High Court of Parliament, and thus possess an inherent jurisdiction.
30 *Kilbourn v. Thompson* 103 US 168 (1881).
31 See Louis Fisher *Constitutional Conflicts Between Congress and the President* (Princeton, Princeton University Press, 1985), p. 190.
32 See James Hamilton *The Power to Probe* (New York, Random House, 1976), pp. 208–9.
33 *Barenblatt v. United States* 360 US 109 (1959).
34 Woodrow Wilson *Congressional Government* (London, Constable, 1914), p. 297.
35 See Schick 'Politics through Law', p. 176.
36 *Immigration and Naturalization Service v. Chadha* 103 Supreme Court 2764 (1983).
37 This is the view taken by Joseph P. Harris *Congressional Control of Adminstration* (Washington DC, Brookings, 1964).
38 *Washington Post*, 10 May 1985, p. 136.
39 Cited in *Congressional Oversight Manual* (Washington DC, CRS, 1984), p. 13.
40 See the debate in Morris S. Ogul *Congress Oversees the Bureaucracy* (Pittsburgh, University of Pittsburgh Press, 1976), ch. 1.

8

The Legislative Process

An understanding of *how* the legislative process in Congress operates is essential to any explanation of *why* particular policy results are obtained. This is because the rules governing the introduction, consideration and discussion of proposals are not neutral but favour certain legislative outcomes. As Representative John D. Dingell (Democrat, Michigan) has stated: 'If you let me write procedure and I let you write substance, I'll screw you every time.'[1] In other words, process and policy are intimately connected. By setting the 'rules of the game', the legislative process both delineates what can or cannot be done, and necessitates particular strategies if success is to be achieved.[2] This point is the subject of an inspired piece of congressional doggerel:

> The Clerk's reading a bill
> when an eager young pill
> bounces up and moves to amend,
> which all comes to naught,
> he didn't move when he ought,
> and all that he did was offend.[3]

Just as it would be impossible to play chess without knowing the rules governing the movement of the pieces, so it would be impossible to understand Congress's response to public problems without a knowledge of the way in which the legislative process operates.

Although the precise details of the legislative process have evolved over time in response to the changing demands of Congress's membership, the constitutional design of the institution has tended to promote a way of doing things which has been remarkably persistent. Writing in 1829, one British traveller observed that the Americans had taken 'the principle of democracy . . . and applied it to a legislative body'. Any legislator had 'the privilege to bring forward at any moment, such measures as suit his fancy'.[4] Four years later, another British observer wrote:

the number of amendments had now become very great, and the accumulation of obstacles was increasing with every speech. I was assured – and from the tone of the debate, I have no doubt it was so – that a majority was decidedly in favour of the . . . measure, but minor discrepancies of opinion were found to be irreconcilable . . . the result was that . . . no money was granted at all, and the matter left for debate in another Congress.[5]

The Constitution's failure to define leadership powers, its prohibition on executive officials serving in the legislature and its implicit recognition of the equality of individual representatives and senators, have tended to produce a very open legislative process. It is this common institutional thread which links one Congress to another.

THE PROCESS

The legislative process begins with the introduction of a bill. Unlike the British House of Commons, which has strict rules governing who may introduce a bill, the introduction of legislation in Congress is open to any member.[6] In the House of Representatives the member merely has to hand the proposed bill to the Clerk of the House or place it in a mahogany box called the 'hopper'. Senators may introduce bills from the floor during the 'morning hour' – the first two hours of the legislative day – when business is not subject to debate. Alternatively, they may hand them in to the Clerk of the Senate.

Although a considerable proportion of the legislation dealt with by Congress is initiated by the Executive and the member of Congress who introduces it acts merely as a 'sponsor', there is still considerable freedom for individuals to introduce their own proposals. Assistance with drafting legislation may be provided by interest groups, or by the House or Senate Offices of Legislative Counsel. Originally known as the Legislative Drafting Service, the latter were created in 1918 to provide support for committees, but since then have had their responsibilities widened.[7] Both the House Office of Legislative Counsel, and its counterpart in the Senate, now provide services for individual members. Their lawyers will rewrite proposals in appropriate language and search for precedents or existing laws dealing with the same subject. As such they provide an invaluable service which frees members of Congress from too great a dependence upon either the Executive or interest groups.

Once a bill has been introduced it is numbered and referred to a committee. The task of referral is theoretically in the hands of the Speaker of the House of Representatives and the President *Pro Tempore* of the Senate, but in practice tends to be done by the parliamentarian of each chamber.[8]

Most referrals are uncontroversial as the jurisdictions of the committees are clearly defined by the rules of each chamber, public laws and procedure. Occasionally, a measure will be ambiguously worded by its sponsor in order to maintain some flexibility in its referral to a committee. In this way, the measure may be referred to a sympathetic rather than an unsympathetic committee. For example, the 1963 Civil Rights Bill was drafted slightly differently for each chamber so that it could be referred to the Judiciary Committee in the House and the Commerce Committee in the Senate, and thus by-pass committees dominated by southern Democrats opposed to the measure. If the content of a measure is deemed to overlap the jurisdictions of two or more committees it may be referred to more than one committee. As might be expected, the increased use of omnibus measures during the 1980s has led to a concommitant increase in the number of multiple referrals.

The work of the committees is at the heart of the legislative process. Operating as 'little legislatures' the committees may hold hearings, offer amendments, rewrite and finally report or approve a measure. Alternatively, they may fail to consider it at all: effectively killing the proposal. In fact, only a fraction of the bills referred to committees are eventually reported. For example, of the 8,104 measures introduced into the House in the 98th Congress (1983–4) only 983, or 12.13 per cent, were reported.[9] Similarly, of the 3,454 measures introduced into the Senate in the 98th Congress, only 835, or 24.17 per cent, were reported.[10] Essentially, the committees act both as refining and screening devices. They provide forums for the detailed discussion of legislation, and ensure that bills with only limited support do not progress any further.

Having been reported out of a committee the next stage is for a bill to be placed on a legislative calendar. There are five calendars in the House: bills which raise or spend money are assigned to the Union Calendar; all other major bills are assigned to the House Calendar; uncontroversial bills are assigned to the Consent Calendar; private immigration bills or claims against the government are assigned to the Private Calendar and motions to discharge committees from further consideration of legislation are assigned to the Discharge Calendar. The Senate has only two calendars: the Executive Calendar, on which treaties and executive nominations are listed; and the Calendar of Business, to which all legislation is passed. There is no guarantee that either chamber will debate legislation placed on the calendars, and the procedures for obtaining floor action vary in each chamber. With its twin traditions of unlimited debate and an open amending process, floor debate in the Senate is less rigorously controlled than in the House where each measure will normally be granted a 'rule' by the Rules Committee detailing the conditions of debate.

Table 8.1 *Number of presidential vetoes, 87th to 99th Congresses*

Congress	No. of regular vetoes	No. of pocket vetoes	Total no. of vetoes	No. of vetoes overridden
87th	11	9	20	0
88th	5	4	9	0
89th	10	4	14	0
90th	2	6	8	0
91st	7	4	11	2
92nd	6	14	20	2
93rd	27	12	39	5
94th	32	5	37	8
95th	6	13	19	0
96th	7	5	12	2
97th	9	6	15	2
98th	9	15	24	2
99th	13	7	20	2

Sources: Roger H. Davidson and Thomas Kephart *Indicators of House of Representatives Workload and Activity* (Washington DC, CRS, 1985), p. 64. *Congressional Quarterly Almanac*, 1986, p. 6.

Article I, Section 7 of the Constitution dictates that the House and Senate must pass bills in identical form before they can be sent to the President for his signature. To reconcile any differences between the House and Senate versions of a bill a conference committee is formed to search for a compromise. Once a compromise is reached it is submitted to both chambers for a vote without further amendment. If either chamber rejects the conference report, then a new conference may be called or another bill introduced. If accepted, the compromise bill is sent to the President for his approval or disapproval. Should the President return the measure to Congress without his signature his veto may be overriden provided two-thirds of both chambers concur.[11] If a President neither signs a bill nor returns it to Congress within ten days it also becomes law so long as Congress has not adjourned. Should Congress adjourn within the ten days, however, the bill is lost in what is known as a 'pocket-veto'.[12]

The number of bills vetoed by President has fluctuated considerably over the past twenty-five years in a manner which reflects the general state of presidential-congressional relations (see table 8.1). With two-thirds majorities in both chambers needed to override a veto it is a potent weapon in legislative battles. Often the mere threat of a veto will be enough to cause some modification of a proposal. The move towards complex omnibus legislative vehicles, however, has slightly undermined the President's position as he does not possess an 'item-veto'. The President must either reject or accept the entire package.

In short, for a bill to become a law it must pass successfully through a number of different decision points (see figure 8.1). At any point in this process the bill is subject to obstruction, modification or defeat. As President Kennedy once stated: 'It is very easy to defeat a bill in Congress. It is much more difficult to pass one.'[13] A similar view of the legislative process was given by the Canadian Ambassador to the United States in 1985 when he noted: 'in the Congress of the US it's never over until it's over. And when it's over it's still not over.'[14] Securing the passage of legislation requires not only a majority in favour of the proposal, but majorities at each decision point. To construct these majorities the supporters of a bill must negotiate with a variety of different actors. This means that the legislative process in Congress tends to be characterized by bargaining and compromise. Issues become blurred and proposals diluted as the wishes of individuals are taken into account. As a result, policy change tends to be incremental. Radical change is difficult to achieve.

THE NATURE OF THE PROCESS

The decentralized nature of the legislative process in the House of Representatives and Senate mirrors the broader political environment in which Congress operates. In particular, the weakness of the political parties means that there is no strong, centralized force able to integrate the various parts of the system. Policy is enacted only when temporary coalitions coalesce around an issue. Although this has led to many criticisms of the 'inefficiency' of Congress, it does ensure that the views of many different interests are taken into account when making public policy. The legislative process ensures that laws are the result of compromise between different factions.

Notes

1 *Congressional Quarterly Weekly Report*, 22 August 1987, p. 1951.

2 See, for example, Walter J. Oleszek *Congressional Procedures and the Policy Process* (Washington DC, Congressional Quarterly Press, 1984), pp. 9–11.

3 Quoted in Donald G. Tacheron and Morris K. Udall *The Job of the Congressman* (Indianapolis, Bobbs-Merril, 1966), p. 193.

4 Captain Basil Hall *Travels in North America in the Years 1827 and 1828* (Edinburgh, Cadell, 1829), vol.III, pp. 25–6.

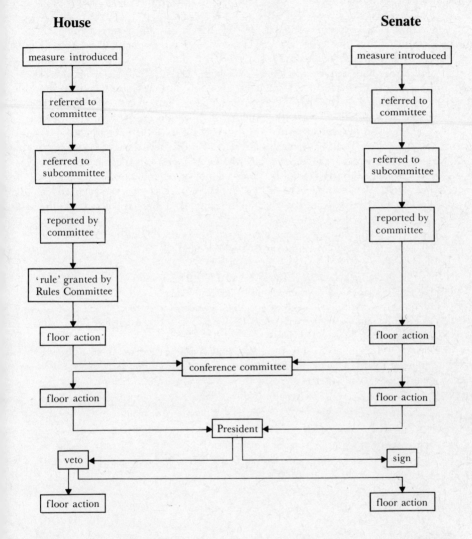

House   **Senate**

Figure 8.1 *How a bill becomes law. (Note that though this is the most typical way in which legislation is enacted into law, there are other methods both more simple and more complicated)*

5 Thomas Hamilton *Men and Manners in America* (Edinburgh, William Blackwood, 1833), vol.II, pp. 40–1.

6 For simplicity legislative proposals are referred to as bills in this chapter. In fact, there are four types of proposals: bills, joint resolutions, concurrent resolutions, and resolutions. There is no real difference between bills and resolutions: both require the approval of both chambers and the signature of the President. Concurrent resolutions are used for measures affecting the operations of both chambers. They must be passed in the same form by both chambers. Resolutions deal with matters entirely within the prerogatives of one chamber. Like concurrent resolutions, they do not have the force of law.

7 The Legislative Drafting Service was created by the Revenue Act (1918).

8 Each chamber has a parliamentarian who is an expert on rules of procedure. The parliamentarian advises the chair on points of order or parliamentary practice. In the 100th Congress (1987–88) there were two parliamentarians in the Senate, one appointed by the Democrats and one appointed by the Republicans.

9 Roger H. Davidson and Thomas Kephart *Indicators of House of Representatives Workload and Activity* (Washington DC, CRS, 1985), p. 26.

10 Ibid. p. 31.

11 In *Missouri Pac. Ry. Co v. Kansas* 248 US 276 (1919) the Supreme Court decided that two-thirds of a quorum sufficed for an override vote. This has been interpreted as two-thirds of those members present and voting.

12 Congress has no opportunity to override a pocket-veto because it has adjourned *sine die*.

13 Donald Bruce Johnson and Jack L. Walker eds 'President John Kennedy Discusses the Presidency' in *The Dynamics of the American Presidency* (New York, John Wiley, 1964), p. 144.

14 Quoted in the *Wall Street Journal*, 29 July 1985.

9

The Committee System

The importance of committees in Congress has long been appreciated. Writing in 1885, for example, Woodrow Wilson noted that: 'Congress in session is Congress on public exhibition, whilst Congress in its committee rooms is Congress at work.'[1] As Wilson recognized, it is in the congressional committees that most of the detailed discussion of legislation and oversight of the Executive Branch takes place. They are the central element of the congressional infrastructure: their organization and functions reflect the much broader political forces to which Congress is subject. Not only are shifting demands for public policy reflected in the creation or abolition of committees, but their internal structure alters with the changing goals of their membership. An examination of the committee system, therefore, is important for two reasons. First, a knowledge of the way committees operate is essential to an understanding of the legislative process. Second, an analysis of the way in which committees have evolved and changed helps illustrate a more general discussion of the dynamics of congressional development. In short, committees are important because in many respects they may be viewed as microcosms of Congress itself.

THE DEVELOPMENT OF THE COMMITTEE SYSTEM

In its conception and in the way it operated the committee system of the early Congresses borrowed much from the British Parliament. Legislative proposals were usually considered first on the floor of the House of Representatives or the Senate, and then referred to special or select committees for detailed drafting. Once their work was completed these committees, like the standing committees in the British Parliament, were dissolved.[2] One study has shown that there were 350 such committees in the 3rd Congress (1793–5) alone; most with only three members.[3] This system of prior consideration by the whole chamber and subsequent referral to temporary committees was predicated upon the belief that legislators were both capable of obtaining, and then evaluating, all the relevant information about an issue without specialized help.[4] This was a point which astounded one early British observer of Congress who wrote:

I can . . . bear testimony to the general information which the whole members of the House of Representatives seem to possess upon all questions . . . It is not as in Britain, where . . . a small number of members only are thoroughly acquainted with it, and the great bulk of those who vote know little or nothing of the subject. At Washington, the whole house are conversant with all business before it on a particular day.[5]

As legislation increased in volume and complexity during the early nineteenth century, however, this assumption began to be questioned. Gradually, permanent or standing committees began to replace the special or select committees and, increasingly, legislation was referred to the new panels prior to consideration by the entire chamber. In other words, the need to cope with an expanding workload, together with the need for specialization, led to the creation of a system of permanent standing committees.[6]

The Emergence of Committees

As the chamber which tended to initiate legislation in the early Congresses, the House was the first to create legislative standing committees. The Claims Committee was created in 1794; Commerce and Manufactures, Revisal and Unfinished Business and Ways and Means in 1795. Four further committees came into being between 1800 and 1810.[7] At this time, the Senate had only four standing committees, all chiefly administrative in nature: the Committee on Enrolled Bills (1789), the Committee on Engrossed Bills (1806), the Committee on the Library (1806) and the Committee on Audit and Control of the Contingent Expenses of the Senate (1807).[8] Between 1810 and 1820, however, both the Senate and the House rapidly expanded their committee systems. In this decade the House created twelve new standing committees, including Judiciary (1813) and Agriculture (1820). The Senate established its first legislative standing committees in December 1816 when twelve were organized, seven of which are still in existence: Armed Services, Commerce, Governmental Affairs, Finance, Foreign Relations, Energy and Natural Resources and Judiciary. By the beginning of the American Civil War the number of committees in the Senate had risen to twenty-two and the number in the House to thirty-four.

Accompanying this increase in numbers prior to the Civil War were two important procedural changes which institutionalized the role of the standing committees in the legislative process. First, the practice of discussing legislation on the floor of the House before referral to a committee finally came to an end in the late 1820s, though it continued in the Senate until the 1860s.[9] This was, in fact, the 'golden age' of Senate floor debate, with proceedings dominated by the likes of John C. Calhoun, Henry Clay and Daniel Webster. Second, the Senate in 1817, and the House in 1822, adopted rules which allowed committees to report a bill without first obtaining the approval of the chamber. Together, these two changes not only gave the committees, particularly in the House, a degree of independence which they had hitherto not enjoyed, but also formalized their role in the legislative process. It became routine to refer bills to committees, and defer to their decisions as they developed an expertise in a particular policy area.

The Era of Rapid Growth

If the first half of the nineteenth century may be viewed as the period when the system of standing committees became firmly established on Capitol Hill, the second half of the century was the era of its most rapid growth. Responding to demands generated by the twin forces of demographic change and the increasing desirability of a congressional career, the number of standing committees in Congress grew at a phenomenal rate. By 1913 there were sixty-one such committees in the House, and no fewer than seventy-four in the Senate (see figure 9.1). Instead of expanding the jurisdictions of existing committees, both the House and the Senate during this period tended to create new committees to meet new policy demands. As a result, committees often had overlapping jurisdictions. Being permanent responses to temporary policy demands, many had no legislative business after an initial flurry of activity, and by the 1900s approximately half never met.[10] Some indication of this lack of purpose can be ascertained from the fact that very few of the committees created in the fifty years from 1870 to 1920 have survived (see table 9.1). Most of the committees from this period of expansion have subsequently been absorbed by other committees or simply abolished.

Although the actual standing committees created between 1870 and 1920 may have been ephemeral, this period represents an important stage in the development of the congressional committee system. In particular, it was during this period that committee chairmen began to control both the flow of legislation to the floor and the debate which followed. So great was their influence that Woodrow Wilson was able to conclude in 1885 that: 'I know not how better to describe our form of government than by calling it a government by the chairmen of the Standing Committees of Congress.'[11] Committee autonomy, however, was limited during this period

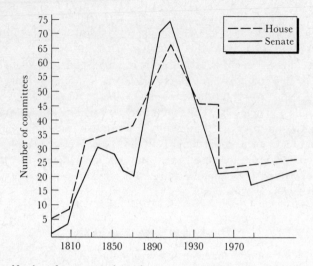

Figure 9.1   *Number of congressional standing committees, 1789–1989. (Note that graphs have been smoothed between points of major change.) (From Stephen S. Smith and Christopher J. Deering* Committees in Congress *(Washington DC, Congressional Quarterly Press, 1984); US House, Select Committee on Committees, 'Committee Reform Amendments of 1974' Report 93rd Congress, 2nd sess., 21 March 1974; US Senate, Temporary Select Committee to Study the Senate Committee System, 'The Senate Committee System, Jurisdictions, Referrals, Numbers and Sizes, and Limitations on Membership' First Staff Report 94th Congress, 2nd sess., 25 July 1976; Congressional Directories)*

by the strong leadership exercised by the likes of Speakers Thomas Reed (1889–91, 1895–9) and Joseph Cannon (1903–11) in the House, and by Nelson Aldrich (1881–1911) in the Senate. By controlling committee assignments and determining which panels should deal with a particular measure, such leaders were able to maintain considerable control over the legislative process. In effect, the parties were the glue which held the bloated committee system together.

The Consolidation of Committee Power

The potential for chaos in such an inflated committee system was obscured for many years by the strong leadership exercised in the House and Senate. Following the Progressive Reforms of the early twentieth century, which undermined the authority of party leaders, the problems of having so many committees with overlapping jurisdictions became apparent, and led to demands for reform.[12] In 1921 the Senate consolidated its seventy-four standing committees into thirty-four standing committees. The consolidation of the committee system in the House was more gradual, but between 1920

Table 9.1   *Dates that current standing committees were created*

House		Senate	
1789	Administration	1789	Rules and Administration
1795	Energy and Commerce		
	Ways and Means		
1805	Interior		
1808	District of Columbia		
	Post Office		
1813	Judiciary		
	Veterans' Affairs		
1816	Government Operations	1816	Commerce
			Governmental Affairs
			Finance
			Foreign Relations
			Armed Services
			Energy/Natural Resources
			Judiciary
1820	Agriculture		
1822	Foreign Affairs		
	Armed Services		
		1825	Agriculture
1837	Public Works	1837	Environment/Public Works
1865	Banking		
	Appropriations		
1867	Education and Labor	1867	Appropriations
		1869	Labor and Human Resources
1880	Rules		
1887	Merchant Marine		
		1913	Banking
1942	Small Business		
		1950	Small Business
1958	Science & Technology		
1967	Official Conduct		
		1970	Veterans' Affairs
1975	Budget	1975	Budget

Note: Only those committees in existence in 1988 are listed. Where committees have been consolidated, the date cited is that of the component committee which was created first.

Sources: Adapted from table in *How Congress Works* (Washington DC, Congressional Quarterly Press, 1983), p. 80; *Congressional Directories*.

and 1940 the number of committees fell from fifty-six to forty-three. Further reform in both chambers occurred in 1946 with the enactment of the Legislative Reorganization Act. By abolishing minor committees and merging those with related functions, this act reduced the number of standing committees in the Senate to fifteen, and the number of standing committees in the House to nineteen. In addition, the Legislative Reorganization Act (1946) also redefined the jurisdictions of committees and attempted to set procedures governing their operations.

The reform of the committee system between 1920 and 1946 not only reduced the number of committees but also increased their power. In the absence of strong party leadership, and bolstered by expanded jurisdictions and the development of the seniority system, the autonomy of the committees and the power of their chairmen were enhanced. The fact that the majority party member with the most years of continuous service on a committee automatically became its chairman meant that little was owed to either party leaders or the President. By the 1950s, so great was the domination of the chairmen that one political scientist was able to claim that:

Just as the standing committees control legislative action, so the chairmen are masters of their committees . . . They arrange the agenda of the committees, appoint the subcommittees, and refer bills to them. They decide what pending measures shall be considered and when, call committee meetings, and decide whether or not to hold hearings and when. They approve lists of scheduled witnesses and authorize staff studies, and preside at committee meetings. They handle reported bills on the floor and participate as principle managers in conference committees. They are in a position to expedite measures they favor and to retard or pigeon-hole those they dislike.[13]

The aura of power surrounding committee chairmen was aptly summed up by Speaker John McCormack (1962–71) when he counselled freshmen: 'Whenever you pass a committee chairman in the House, you bow from the waist. I do.'[14]

Despite several attempts at reform there has been no major reorganization of congressional committees since 1946.[15] The nearest either chamber has come to a major overhaul of its committees occurred in 1977 when the Senate authorized a modest consolidation of its committees. Senate Resolution 4 (1977) reduced the number of standing committees in the Senate from eighteen to fifteen. Otherwise, change has tended to be incremental: the Legislative Reorganization Act (1970) created a Veterans' Affairs Committee in the Senate; the Congressional Budget and Impoundment Act (1974) established Budget Committees in both chambers; and both the House and the Senate have occasionally abolished or created the odd committee. There are currently sixteen standing committees in the

Senate and twenty-two in the House. In fact, rather than attempting to restructure the basic committee system, the most recent reform in Congress has tended to concentrate on how the existing committees *operate*. Although perhaps not so visible as a wholesale consolidation of committees, the institutionalization of subcommittees, challenges to the authority of committee chairmen and changes in the assignment process have significantly affected the operations of the committees and, hence, the legislative process.

SUBCOMMITTEE GOVERNMENT

It is not clear when the first subcommittees were created in Congress. Writing in 1915, Representative Burton K. French reported that approximately thirty-five House committees and twenty-seven Senate committees had established formal subcommittees and were using them on a regular basis.[16] By the time of the Legislative Reorganization Act (1946) there were an estimated ninety-seven House subcommittees and thirty-four Senate subcommittees in existence.[17] Although initially reducing the number of subcommittees in the House to sixty-two, the consolidation of standing committees caused by the 1946 reorganization eventually spawned an explosion in the number of subcommittees in both chambers (see table 9.2). By the 85th Congress (1957–8) there were 114 subcommittees in the House and eighty-five in the Senate. Ten years later there were 135 subcommittees in the House and ninety-eight in the Senate. Many of these new subcommittees mirrored the jurisdictions of previous committees which had been abolished by the 1946 act. Others were created as a response to new policy demands, particularly the emergence of more complex issues which required greater policy specialization.

The creation of a large network of subcommittees following the Legislative Reorganization Act (1946) did not automatically lead to a dispersal of power in Congress. Rather the full committee chairmen tended to use the subcommittees to enhance their own authority. They were able to create subcommittees, determine their membership and define their jurisdictions in accordance with their own wishes. By chairing a subcommittee, the full committee chairman and a small group of trusted colleagues could control the consideration of legislation: effectively limiting participation to two or three members.[18] This fact meant that the subcommittees became a natural target of a new generation of congressmen obtaining office in the 1960s and 1970s. Eager to make a quick name for themselves to further their chances of re-election, they sought immediate access to the policy-making

Table 9.2   *Number of subcommittees of standing committees in Congress,*
1945–1986

Congress	House	Senate
79th (1945–6)	97	57
80th (1947–8)	102	61
81st (1949–50)	62	63
82nd (1951–2)	73	65
83rd (1953–4)	81	66
84th (1955–6)	85	87
85th (1957–8)	114	85
86th (1959–60)	120	87
87th (1961–2)	125	88
88th (1963–4)	121	85
89th (1965–6)	125	92
90th (1967–8)	135	98
91st (1969–70)	130	101
92nd (1971–2)	120	115
93rd (1973–4)	125	127
94th (1975–6)	149	122
95th (1977–8)	146	96
96th (1979–80)	150	90
97th (1981–2)	140	101
98th (1983–4)	139	102
99th (1985–6)	140	88

Note: From the 94th Congress onwards, the figures for subcommittees
in the House of Representatives include Budget Committee Task
Forces.
Sources: Roger H. Davidson and Thomas Kephart *Indicators of House
of Representatives Workload and Activity* (Washington DC, CRS, 1985),
p. 36; Roger H. Davidson and Thomas Kephart *Indicators of
Senate Activity and Workload* (Washington DC, CRS, 1985), p. 32;
Congressional Directories.

process.[19] Such access was most easily obtained through reform of the
subcommittee system.

Subcommittee Reforms

The first reform of the subcommittee system occurred in 1971 when the
Democratic caucus in the House voted in favour of a rule change which

prohibited members from chairing more than one legislative subcommittee. This ensured that committee chairmen could no longer chair several subcommittees. The next reform occurred in 1973 when the Democratic caucus adopted a 'subcommittee bill of rights'.[20] This established a Democratic 'caucus' on each committee and gave these caucuses the authority to select committee chairmen, define subcommittee jurisdictions and set subcommittee budgets. In effect, the 'bill of rights' was a declaration of autonomy from both the full committee and its chairman.[21] The authority of committee chairmen was weakened further in 1974 when the Democrats adopted a rule change which required all committees with more than twenty members to establish at least four subcommittees. This rule change was directed specifically at Ways and Means which, under the sixteen-year chairmanship of Wilbur Mills (Democrat, Arkansas), had not established any subcommittees. Strong, independent, subcommittees were intended to undermine Mills's power. In a similar move aimed at undermining the authority of senior Democrats on the House Appropriations Committee, who monopolized the important subcommittees handling the budgets for defence, agriculture, labour, health, education and welfare, the Democratic caucus in 1975 specified that no Democrat could become a member of a second subcommittee on any full committee until every member of the full committee had chosen one subcommittee position. A further limitation on subcommittee assignments was adopted in 1979 when the caucus agreed to limit each Democrat to service on five subcommittees.

Mirroring many of the reforms adopted by the House during the 1970s, the Senate also moved to restructure its subcommittee system. Instead of proceeding by stages, however, the Senate reformed its practices in one reorganization. Senate Resolution 4 (1977) contained provisions which prohibited a senator from serving as a chairman of more than one subcommittee on each committee of which he or she was a member, and limited senators to membership of just three subcommittees of any major standing committee. Finally, although it was not made a formal requirement, the Senate adopted a proposal stating that no member of a committee should receive a second subcommittee assignment until all members of the committee had received their first assignment.

The Problems of Subcommittee Government

The effect of the decade of reform in the House, and the passage of Senate Resolution 4 (1977) in the Senate, was to institutionalize subcommittees in both chambers: a development which had a number of important consequences. First, the new autonomy of the subcommittees undermined the authority of the committee chairmen. This, together with the emergence of subcommittees as important centres of legislative activity, further fragmented decision-making in Congress. Second, the enhanced role of subcommittees provided interest groups with an additional point of entry into the political process. Finally, the proliferation of subcommittees resulted in increased demands upon members. More subcommittees meant more assignments, more hearings and more legislation to be drafted.

Recognition of the problems associated with subcommittee growth was acknowledged by the House Select Committee on Committees, chaired by Representative Jerry Patterson (Democrat, California), in 1980. The report of the Patterson Committee noted that: 'On no other issue concerning committee system revision has the Select Committee on Committees found greater agreement on the part of Members, staff, and students of Congress than that there are too many subcommittees in the House and that Members have too many subcommittee assignments.'[22] The Patterson Committee proposed limiting each member to a maximum of five subcommittee assignments and limiting each committee, with the exception of Appropriations, to a maximum of six subcommittees. The first proposal merely echoed the 1979 decision of the Democratic caucus, but it was not until January 1981 that a decision was taken regarding the number of subcommittees each committee could create. In a vote, the Democratic caucus agreed to limit the number of subcommittees which the Rules Committee and Ways and Means could establish to six, and limited all other committees, except Appropriations, to a maximum of eight. Appropriations was allowed to retain its thirteen subcommittees.

In a similar expression of concern about the consequences of the proliferation of subcommittees in the Senate, the Temporary Select Committee to Study the Senate Committee System, chaired by Senator Dan Quayle (Republican, Indiana), concluded in 1984 that: 'if senators will agree to reduce their committee assignments, our committees will be able to perform their duties and the Senate as a whole will be taken more seriously as a reliable and informed policymaker.'[23] The committee suggested the elimination of thirty subcommittees, but its proposals were not acted upon. In response to the Quayle Committee's findings, however, the Senate did abolish fourteen subcommittees in the 99th Congress (1985–6).

The failure of both the House and the Senate to reform significantly the subcommittee system, despite growing evidence of the problems caused by a fragmented legislative process, is testimony to the difficulties in engendering reform in either chamber which is perceived as infringing upon the prerogatives of the membership. Subcommittees provide senators and representatives with both the resources and the opportunity to make policy. With an electoral environment which stresses individual achievement, these facilities are too important to give up for the sake of institutional efficiency.

In short, there is little incentive for members of Congress to change the system: it serves their electoral requirements as it stands.

COMMITTEE CHAIRMEN

The 'institutionalization' of the subcommittees during the 1970s was clearly connected with a more general assault upon the authority of the chairmen of the standing committees. Through the establishment of autonomous subcommittees with staff of their own, junior members in both chambers hoped to undermine the power of committee chairmen. To reinforce these efforts, two other major reform initiatives were undertaken. First, the seniority system was challenged. Second, the activities of the committees were opened to public scrutiny. By both threatening the basis of their power and making their actions visible to people outside Congress, these reforms helped erode the position of dominance previously maintained by the chairmen.

The Seniority System

The authority of standing committee chairmen between 1910 and 1970 was predicated upon the strict operation of the seniority principle, under which the member of the majority party with the longest record of service on the committee became the chairman. With seniority also went greater office space, more resources and more respected opinions. Although there has been some debate about the precise origins of this principle, the automatic selection of chairmen according to longevity became firmly established in both chambers during the first two decades of the twentieth century.[24] Such a method of selecting committee chairmen, unique to the US Congress, was justified by its supporters on a number of grounds. It was suggested that it offered an attainable ambition for any member of Congress; prevented internal strife by forestalling competition for chairmanships; rewarded experience and, perhaps most importantly, prevented too much power from being centralized in the hands of the party leadership.[25] On the other hand, the use of seniority to determine chairmanships insulated chairmen from the demands of the other members of the committee: it gave them power without responsibility. It also provided no means of removing inadequate or senile leaders, and denied junior members access to power and resources. Of all these criticisms, it was the last which lay behind the demands for reform in the 1970s. Faced with an increasingly volatile electoral environment, junior members of both chambers felt that they could ill afford to wait for the benefits of seniority to accrue to them. Rather, they required immediate access to the advantages normally afforded to senior members only.

As a result of the pressure exerted by junior members, both the House and the Senate adopted a number of reforms between 1970 and 1975 which undermined the *theoretical* basis of the seniority principle. In January 1971 the Democratic caucus in the House accepted a recommendation that the Democratic Committee on Committees need not have to follow seniority when nominating committee chairmen. If ten or more Democrats disagreed with the Committee on Commmittees' nominations then the issue would be decided by a vote of the caucus. In 1971, the Republicans also agreed to allow the Republican Committee on Committees leeway to use. criteria other than seniority when nominating ranking members of House committees. If seniority was waived by the Committee on Committees then the Republican Conference would have to vote on the nomination. The next modification of the seniority principle occurred in 1973 when the Republicans in the Senate adopted a rule which allowed the Republican members of each committee to elect their own ranking member, subject to ratification by the Republican Conference. Further changes were initiated in January 1975 when House Democrats adopted a rule which required all committee chairmen and the subcommittee chairmen of the Appropriations Committee to be elected by secret ballot. In a similar move, Democrats in the Senate adopted a rule which required a secret ballot on nominations for a chair if one-fifth of the Democrats in the Senate so requested.

In an effort to show that these reforms were not intended to be 'cosmetic' House Democrats in 1975 voted to oust three incumbent chairmen: Representative W. R. Poage (Democrat, Texas) of the Agriculture Committee; Representative F. Edward Herbert (Democrat, Louisiana) of Armed Services; and Representative Wright Patman (Democrat, Texas) of the Banking and Currency Committee. Another chairman, Representative Wilbur Mills (Democrats, Arkansas) resigned when he realized that he would not be re-elected as chairman.[26] The breach of the seniority principle suggested by these challenges was confirmed when the Democrats selected Representative Henry Reuss (Democrat, Wisconsin) to head the Banking Committee. Reuss lacked the seniority of many other Democrats on the committee. In January 1985 Representative Lee Aspin *(Democrat, Wisconsin) was also selected over more senior Democrats to be chairman of the Armed Services Committee after House Democrats has voted to remove the incumbent chairman Representative Melvin Price (Democrat, Illinois). Aspin himself was ousted as Armed Services chairman in a vote of the party caucus in January 1987, but less than two weeks later was restored to his position in a vote for the vacancy created by his original removal.[27]

To date there has been no challenge to seniority in the Senate. Indeed, in Janury 1987 Senate Republicans voted to uphold the principle of seniority when they confirmed Senator Jesse Helms (Republican, North Carolina), rather than Senator Richard Lugar (Republican, Indiana), as ranking member of the Foreign Relations Committee. In 1985 Lugar, the second ranking member of Foreign Relations behind Helms had become chairman of the committee after the latter had opted to be chairman of the Agriculture Committee. Following the 1986 election, when the Republicans lost their majority status, Helms sought to reclaim his seniority on Foreign Relations, and beat Lugar for the position in a twenty-four to seventeen vote of the Republican Conference.

Government in the Sunshine

Despite this apparent adherence to the seniority principle, chairmen in the Senate, like their counterparts in the House, know that the party caucus and their colleagues on the committee *can* vote to remove them. This threat has had a restraining influence upon their activities: it has added responsibility to the power they possess. A further restraint upon the activities of the committee chairmen was established with the enactment of 'sunshine' rules which opened up the activities of the committees to public scrutiny. Such changes meant that the actions of the chairmen became more visible. They were seen as an integral part of the 'democratization' of Congress's procedures.

'Sunshine' provisions within the Legislative Reorganization Act (1970) provided for the televising of committee hearings in both the House and the Senate. In 1973 the House adopted rules which opened all committee sessions to the public unless a majority of the committee voted in an open meeting to hold a closed session. The Senate adopted similar rules in 1975. While these reforms may have imposed further restraint upon the activities of the committee chairman, one unintended consequence was to make both chambers more susceptible to pressure from interest groups and constituents. As Representative Dan Rostenkowski (Democrat, Illinois), chairman of the Ways and Means Committee, has pointed out:

When we come to this glorious, open, participatory government, you know, one of my members is sitting there looking at some labor skate and thinking, 'Oh well, how does he want me to vote on this one?' Or the labor guy is running around and pulling him out to say, 'Wait a minute you can't do this.'[28]

Information about a member's position on legislation became public knowledge, and liable for use in elections campaigns. As a result members of Congress began to conduct their committee work with considerable circumspection, aware that any vote might harm them in their next re-election campaign. The Ways and Means Committee and the subcommittees of the Appropriations Commitee in the House and the Appropriations and Finance Committees in the Senate have even begun to opt for more closed sessions in order to reduce the problem of over-intrusive interest groups.

The enactment of 'sunshine' rules, the undermining of seniority and the 'institutionalization' of subcommittees all worked to reduce the authority of committee chairmen. Generally speaking, chairmen now need to bargain and negotiate with other members of the committee, particularly subcommittee chairmen. Care must be taken, however, before totally dismissing the position of the modern chairmen. As the leader of the committee the chairman still has considerable influence over the legislative process.

THE ASSIGNMENT PROCESS

The central position of the committees in the legislative process means that the manner in which assignments to the various panels are made is extremely important to the individual senator or representative. Without a place on the appropriate committee the individual's ability to influence policy is restricted. It is through their committee work that most members make their reputations.[29] This is particularly the case in the House which has less of a tradition of floor debate than the Senate. At the beginning of each congressional session, therefore, there is considerable competition for committee seats. Freshmen make their preferences known, and more senior members may attempt to move to more prestigious panels.

Committee Preferences

In a seminal study of six committees in the House of Representatives, Richard F. Fenno identified three goals which influence an individual's committee preferences: the opportunity of improving chances of re-election, the possibility of shaping good public policy and the chance to achieve power and influence within the chamber.[30] Subsequent studies have since identified similar goals governing committee preferences in the Senate.[31] Although the relative importance of these three goals has varied in recent years that of re-election has assumed increasing importance.[32] Both representatives and senators have increasingly preferred committee asssignments which may further their chances of re-election. In other words, they wish to serve on committees whose jurisdictions cover policy areas pertinent to their constituents. Members representing farming areas, for example, have sought seats on the Agriculture Committees, while most members covet seats on the Appropriations Committees because of their control over spending. Obviously, the attractiveness of specific committees will vary as the political environment changes. During the 1980s with an increased emphasis on budgetary matters, seats on the taxing and spending committees have become more important. As Representative Thomas J. Downey (Democrat, New York), a member of the Ways and Means Committee, has stated: 'Life outside these committees can be pretty dreary. It's like a coal mine – only the people in the car have access to coal.'[33] Seats on the Judiciary Committees, on the other hand, have become less desirable as highly controversial issues such as busing, abortion and school prayer have become more prominent.

Reform of the Assignment Process

The fact that committee assignments are often the key to congressional careers means that the method employed to fill committee places has become the focus for reform when significant numbers of individuals find that their requirements are not being met. A changing set of electoral needs, or a new generation of legislators, may well generate demands for reform of the assignment process as existing criteria for the placement of individuals are superseded by events. In this way, changing membership needs provide a link between the broader political environment and legislative practices. Changes in the external environment are reflected in new membership goals which, in turn, may lead to reform of legislative processes. Knowledge of this dynamic helps explain why changes in the assignment process have occurred.

From 1790 to 1911 the appointment of members to committees in the House was the responsibility of the Speaker. In making appointments the Speaker was guided by certain criteria, the most significant of which was the fact that the committees had to be bipartisan, but generally speaking their freedom of action was considerable and served to buttress their power.[34] Following the Progressive revolt against Speaker Cannon in 1910 control over appointments passed from the Speaker to the House. A rule change adopted by the Democrats in 1911 provided for the selection of committee members by the full House. Over the next decade both parties vested power over committee assignments in the hands of a committee on committees. The Democratic Committee on Committees was composed of the Democratic members of the Ways and Means Committee, while the Republican Committee on Committees was made up of one member of each state party delegation. In December 1974, as part of the effort by junior Democrats to undermine the authority of committee chairmen, the Democratic caucus voted to transfer the power to make committee assignments from the Committee on Committees to the Steering and Policy Committee which is composed of eight members chosen by the Speaker, twelve regionally elected members and the party and committee leaders who sit as *ex officio* members.

In its early years control over committee assignments in the Senate had at various times been the prerogative of the entire membership, the Vice-President, and the President *Pro Tempore*. By the late 1870s, however, both parties had established committees on committees.[35] Although the function of the Democratic Committee on Committees was taken over by the Democratic Steering Committee in 1947, and the precise method of choosing the membership of the two committees has varied over the years, they are still the formal mechanisms through which committee places are assigned in the Senate. The Republican Committee on Committees currently has approximately fifteen members, who are appointed by the chairman of the Republican Conference. The Democratic Steering Committee has approximately twenty-five members, who are appointed by the Democratic floor leader.

The formal criteria by which the parties assign committee places in both the House and the Senate are relatively simple. Both chambers use a modified form of seniority as the basis for assigning seats. At the beginning of each new Congress, representatives and senators are ranked by party according to their seniority. In the Senate, rank is determined by listing senators according to the date of the start of their service. On those occasions when members begin their service on the same date, previous political experience is taken into account. Members are ranked on the basis of previous service as a senator, representative or governor. If this still does not distinguish between members then a ballot is held. In the House, experience as a senator or governor is not taken into account when determining seniority. Only prior service in the House is used to distinguish between members beginning their service on the same date. Using these rankings, the assignment committees will then begin to fill the committees. On most occasions, serving members of the committees will retain their places; seniority is only used to fill any vacancies.

To ensure a reasonably equitable distribution of assignments, party rules in the House and standing orders in the Senate restrict the number and type of committees on which members may serve. In the House, the Democratic caucus divides the committees into three categories: exclusive, major and nonmajor.[36] Democrats serving on an exclusive committee are prohibited from serving on any other standing committee.[37] Other Democrats may serve on one major and one nonmajor or two nonmajor committees. All are guaranteed a seat on either an exclusive or major committee. Republicans divide the committees into major and minor panels in much the same way as the Democrats, and may serve on one major and one minor committee, or on at least two minor committees. In the Senate, Majority Leader Senator Lyndon Johnson (Democrat, Texas) instituted the so-called 'Johnson Rule' in 1953 which prohibited any Democrat from receiving a second assignment on the Appropriations, Armed Services, Finance or Foreign Relations Committees until all party members had received one assignment on one of these panels. Senate Republicans adopted similar rules, first informally in 1959, and then through the Republican Conference in 1965. Further regulations governing committee assignments in the Senate were adopted in 1977 with the passage of Senate Resolution 4 (1977). These rules divided Senate committees into major and minor committees.[38] Senators were permitted to serve on two major committees and one minor committee.

Increases in the Number of Assignments

Although modifications in the seniority principle have made places on major committees in both the House and the Senate available to junior members, the insistent pressure of constituency demands has also led to efforts to obtain *more*, not just *better*, assignments.[39] Since the 79th Congress (1945–6), when the average size of a standing committee in the House was 20.02 members, and the average size of a standing committee in the Senate was 14.9 members, the size of the committees has grown almost inexorably (see table 9.3). The average standing committee in the House is now approximately 75 per cent larger than it was in 1946. In the Senate, the growth in the size of the committees has been less spectacular, but the average standing committee is still approximately 20 per cent larger than it was in 1946.

The result of the growth in the size of the committees, together with the proliferation of subcommittees, has been an increase in the number of committee assignments for each member (table 9.4). The consequences of the growth in the number of committee assignments held by each representative and senator are fairly obvious. More assignments mean more meetings, hearings and scheduling of problems. With its smaller membership, these problems have been felt most acutely in the Senate, and have led to attempts at reform. Senate Resolution 4 (1977) reduced the average number of committee assignments from 15.57 to 10.54, but the numbers began to creep up again almost immediately. Reporting in 1985, the Quayle Committee detailed the implications of this growth:

When senators acquire additional committee and subcommittee commitments, it becomes increasingly difficult for them to attend all the meetings scheduled for each of their panels. This situation frustrates not only each individual senator, but the chairmen of committees when they try to muster a quorum to conduct business.[40]

Table 9.3   *Average size of House and Senate standing committees, 87th to 99th Congresses*

Congress	House	Senate
87th (1961–2)	29.4	15.0
88th (1963–4)	29.5	16.0
89th (1965–6)	30.1	15.6
90th (1967–8)	29.5	15.8
91st (1969–70)	30.1	15.3
92nd (1971–2)	31.8	14.5
93rd (1973–4)	32.5	14.3
94th (1975–6)	35.4	14.2
95th (1977–8)	35.2	16.2
96th (1979–80)	34.6	16.8
97th (1981–2)	34.2	17.6
98th (1983–4)	34.7	18.4
99th (1985–6)	35.5	17.6

Sources: Roger H. Davidson and Thomas Kephart *Indicators of House of Representatives Workload and Activity*, p. 38; Roger H. Davidson and Thomas Kephart *Indicators of Senate Activity and Workload*, p. 37.

Acting upon some of the Quayle Committee's recommendations, the Senate managed to reduce slightly the number of assignments each member held in the 99th Congress. Such a marginal change, however, had little impact in addressing the problems identified by the Quayle Committee.

THE MODERN COMMITTEE SYSTEM

An explanation of why neither the House nor the Senate has been able to resolve the problems posed by multiple committee assignments can be found in the dynamics of congressional development. The committee system in Congress has developed in response to the changing demands of its membership. Thus, recent changes in the position of committee chairmen, the institutionalization of subcommittees and the proliferation of assignments may be viewed as a consequence of changes in the needs of Congress's membership. Although these developments have created a number of problems, including scheduling difficulties and a general fragmentation of power, there is little real pressure for further reform because the current

Table 9.4 *Average number of committee assignments in the House and Senate, 87th to 99th Congresses*

Congress	House	Senate
87th (1961–2)	4.29	10.30
88th (1963–4)	4.46	11.03
89th (1965–6)	4.71	12.32
90th (1967–8)	5.01	12.89
91st (1969–70)	5.12	13.36
92nd (1971–2)	5.36	14.63
93rd (1973–4)	5.70	15.69
94th (1975–6)	6.15	15.57
95th (1977–8)	6.27	10.54
96th (1979–80)	6.15	10.74
97th (1981–2)	5.81	11.19
98th (1983–4)	6.26	11.95
99th (1985–6)	6.45	10.75

Note: Includes assignments to standing committees, subcommittees and select, special and joint committees.
Sources: Roger H. Davidson and Thomas Kephart *Indicators of House of Representatives Workload and Activity*, p. 37; Roger H. Davidson and Thomas Kephart *Indicators of Senate Activity and Workload*, p. 35.

system gives members what they want: access to the policy process and the opportunity to benefit their constituencies. In other words, personal needs tend to take precedence over more general institutional needs.

Notes

1 Woodrow Wilson *Congressional Government* (London, Constable, 1914), p. 79.
2 Confusingly, standing committees in the British Parliament are temporary panels, created to consider a specific legislative measure. In contrast, select committees in the House of Commons are permanent bodies concerned with oversight. In the US Congress this usage is reversed. Standing committees are permanent and select committees temporary. The American terms seem, perhaps, more logical.
3 Lauros G. McConachie *Congressional Committees* (New York, Burt Franklin, reprint of 1898 ed, 1973), pp. 124–5.
4 See Steven S. Smith and Christopher J. Deering *Committees in Congress* (Washington DC, Congressional Quarterly Press, 1984), p. 10.
5 James Stuart *Three Years in North America* (Edinburgh, Cadell, 1832), vol. II, pp. 45–6.

6 By the 100th Congress (1987–8) there were only five select or special committees in the Senate: Ethics, Indian Affairs, Intelligence, Aging and Secret Military Assistance to Iran and the Nicaraguan Opposition. There were six select or special committees in the House: Aging, Children, Hunger, Intelligence, Narcotics and Covert Arms Transactions with Iran. There were also four Joint Committees made up of members from both chambers: Economic, Library, Printing and Taxation.

7 US House of Representatives, Select Committee on Committees, 'Committee Reform Amendments of 1974' *Report* 93rd Congress, 2nd sess., 21 March 1974, appendix A. The first standing committee to be created in the House was the Committee on Elections (1789). This committee, however, was concerned with internal administrative matters, not the consideration of legislation.

8 US Senate, Temporary Select Committee to Study the Senate Committee System, 'The Senate Committee System, Jurisdictions, Referrals, Numbers and Sizes, and Limitations on Membership' *First Staff Report* 94th Congress, 2nd sess., 25 July 1976, p. 11.

9 Joseph Cooper 'The Origins of the Standing Committees and the Development of the Modern House' *Rice University Studies* (56:3), p. 116.

10 Chang-Wei Chiu *The Speaker of the House of Representatives Since 1896* (New York, Columbia University Press, 1928), p. 311.

11 Wilson *Congressional Government*, p. 102.

12 See ch. 3 for details of the revolt against Speaker Cannon.

13 George Galloway *The Legislative Process in Congress* (New York, Thomas Y. Crowell, 1953), p. 289.

14 *Wall Street Journal*, 3 May 1979, p. 1.

15 For a discussion of the attempts to reform the committee system see Leroy N. Rieselbach *Congressional Reform* (Washington DC, Congressional Quarterly Press, 1986), pp. 46–7, 64–6, 68.

16 Burton K. French 'Subcommittees of Congress' *American Political Science Review* (February), 1915, pp. 68–92.

17 Galloway *The Legislative Process*, p. 594.

18 See Smith and Deering *Committees in Congress*, pp. 28–9.

19 See Roger H. Davidson 'Subcommittee Government: New Channels for Policy Making' in Thomas E. Mann and Norman J. Ornstein eds *The New Congress* (Washington DC, American Enterprise Institute, 1981), pp. 106–8.

20 See David W Rohde 'Committee Reform in the House of Representatives' *Annals* (411), 1974, pp. 39–47.

21 Rieselbach *Congressional Reform*, p. 50.

22 US House of Representatives, Select Committee on Committees, 'Limitations on the Number of Subcommittees and Subcommittee Assignments' *Committee Print* 96th Congress, 2nd sess., 1980, p. 1.

23 US Senate, Temporary Select Committee to Study the Senate Committee System, *Report* 98th Congress, 2nd sess., 1984, p. 5.

24 See Nelson W. Polsby 'The Institutionalisation of the House of Representatives' *American Political Science Review* (March), 1968, pp. 160–4 and David J. Rothman

Politics and Power: The US Senate 1869–1901 (Cambridge, Mass., Harvard University Press, 1966), p. 51.

25 See Kenneth Bradshaw and David Pring *Parliament and Congress* (London, Quartet, 1981), p. 241.

26 See Joseph K. Unekis and Leroy N. Rieselbach *Congressional Committee Politics* (New York, Praeger, 1984), pp. 114–15.

27 See *Congressional Quarterly Weekly Report*, 10 January 1987, p. 83 and *Congressional Quarterly Weekly Report*, 24 January 1987, p. 134.

28 *Congressional Quarterly Weekly Report*, 23 May 1987, p. 1059.

29 See Charles S. Bullock 'US Senate Committee Assignments: Preferences, Motivations, and Sources' *American Journal of Political Science* (November), 1985, p. 789.

30 Richard F. Fenno *Congressmen in Committees* (Boston, Little, Brown, 1973).

31 See, for example, Bullock 'US Senate Committee Assignments', p. 795.

32 Roger H. Davidson 'Congressional Committees as Moving Targets' *Legislative Studies Quarterly* (February), 1986, p. 21.

33 *Congressional Quarterly Weekly Report*, 3 January 1987, p. 19.

34 The principle that the committees were to be bipartisan, but weighted in favour of the majority party, was established in the early Congresses. See George Galloway *Congress At the Crossroads* (New York, Thomas Y. Crowell, 1946), pp. 127, 137.

35 The Republicans established a committee on committees during the Civil War; the Democrats followed suit in 1879.

36 The committee categories are as follows:

exclusive	Appropriations, Ways and Means, Rules.
major	Agriculture, Armed Services, Banking, Education, Foreign Affairs, Energy, Judiciary, Public Works.
nonmajor	Budget, District of Columbia, Government Operations, Administration, Interior, Merchant Marine, Post Office, Science and Technology, Small Business, Veterans' Affairs.

37 Members of the Ways and Means Committee may also sit on the Budget Committee.

38 *Major* committees in the Senate are: Agriculture, Appropriations, Armed Services, Banking, Commerce, Energy, Environment, Finance, Foreign Relations, Governmental Affairs, Human Resources and Judiciary. *Minor* committees are: Rules, Veterans' Affairs and Small Businesses.

39 See Davidson 'Congressional Committees as Moving Targets', p. 23.

40 US Senate, Temporary Select Committee to Study the Senate Committee System, *Report* 98th Congress, 2nd sess., 1984, p. 7.

10

Floor Activity

The activity which takes place on the floors of the House of Representatives and the Senate is probably the most visible aspect of Congress at work.[1] It also provides a useful illustration of both the impact that processes have on policy outcomes, and the institutional differences between the House and the Senate. Not only will the terms of debates, amendment and voting affect the possibility of legislative success, but differences in the floor procedures of the two chambers reflect their different constitutional design. With its smaller membership and greater deference to the wishes of individual members, the Senate has, for example, a much more open amending process and opportunities for debate than the much larger House. An understanding of floor procedures is important, therefore, for two main reasons. First, they are a vital aspect of the legislative process; and second, they highlight institutional differences between the two chambers.

THE HOUSE OF REPRESENTATIVES

Essential in any legislature are procedures which both regulate the flow of legislation to the floor and govern its subsequent progress. Without some regulations detailing such factors as the means by which legislation is to be scheduled for business, the conditions governing its amendment, the limitations on its debate and the procedures for bringing the issue to a vote, the work of the legislature would soon grind to a halt. It is interesting to note, for example, that when the First Congress met in 1789 one of the first rules the House adopted concerned the scheduling of motions, the methods of voting and the conditions of debate.[2] As the House grew in size and its workload increased, so a complex set of rules and procedures were evolved to regulate every aspect of floor activity. More members meant more individuals wishing to take part in debates, and more work meant more legislation to consider. The floor procedures which developed in the House reflected these facts. Out of necessity the scheduling of legislation, and its debate and amendment, became tightly controlled. Some indication of this process can be seen in the struggle to limit obstruction in the chamber.

The first limit on debate in the House was made in 1811 when the chamber approved the motion of the *Previous Question* as a means of invoking cloture. The result of moving and carrying the previous question was to cut off debate and bring the House immediately to a vote on the main question. Although this device was effective in closing debate it could not be used while a member held the floor and was engaged in a personal filibuster. As Henry Clay noted in 1812, moving the previous question 'was nothing more than a declaration of the House that it has heard enough and would proceed to decide'.[3] In an attempt to reduce the potential for a personal filibuster the House adopted a rule in 1841 which placed a limit of one hour on any speech. By this action the chamber ended its tradition of unlimited debate.

Adoption of the 'one hour rule' reduced the opportunity to obstruct legislation by 'talking it to death'. This form of filibuster, however, was only one form of obstruction used in the House. Another was obstruction by amendment: the passage of a bill could be delayed by offering and then discussing numerous amendments to the measure under consideration. To counteract this tactic the House adopted the 'five minute rule' in 1847. This rule restricted a member to five minutes only in explaining his amendment. The next major assault upon obstructionist techniques occurred under Speaker Thomas Reed (1889–91, 1895–9). By constantly demanding roll call votes and refusing to answer their names on quorum calls the minority could delay and even bring business to a halt because of a lack of a quorum. In a series of important rulings Speaker Reed brought an end to these tactics. On 21 January 1890 he informed the House that he would disregard all motions and appeals, even if procedurally correct, if they were intended merely to delay business. On the 30 January 1890 he ruled that those members present but not voting would be counted for the purpose of establishing a quorum. When one member challenged Reed's right to declare him as being present, the Speaker, with impeccable logic, replied: 'The Chair is making a statement of the fact that the gentleman . . . is present. Does he deny it?'[4] The 'Reed rules' not only ended the possibility of persistent filibustering in the House, but also severely weakened the role of the minority in the legislative process. When asked about the rights of the minority Reed retorted: 'The right of the minority is to draw its salaries and its function is to make a quorum.'[5] His close colleague, Representative Joseph Cannon (Republican, Illinois), justified the Reed rules on the following grounds:

I say that a majority under the Constitution is allowed to legislate, and that if a contrary practice has grown up, such practice is unrepublican, undemocratic, against sound policy, and contrary to the Constitution.[6]

It had taken approximately 100 years to establish the control of the majority over floor activity in the House.

The Scheduling of Business

Floor activity in the House begins with the scheduling of business. After being reported out of a committee, each bill is placed on one of the four legislative calendars used by the House of Representatives. Bills 'raising revenue, general appropriations bills and bills of a public character directly or indirectly appropriating money or property' are placed on the *Union Calendar*. Major public bills 'not raising revenue nor directly or indirectly appropriating money or property' are placed on the *House Calendar*. Non-controversial bills are placed on the *Consent Calendar*, and private bills dealing with immigration requests or claims against the government are placed on the *Private Calendar*. The number of private bills enacted by Congress has declined dramatically in recent years as legal changes have opened up other avenues for the redress of grievances. For example, the Federal Tort Claims Act (1946) allows citizens to sue the government in federal courts on negligence cases, thereby diminishing the need for private bills. In the 99th Congress (1985–6) only twenty-four such bills were enacted, compared with 6,249 between 1905 and 1907. As Representative Barney Frank (Democrat, Massachusetts) has noted, a private bill is now 'an extreme pressure valve. It is used in a very small number of cases to correct a mistake because there is no other way to correct it'.[7] The House has one further calendar, the *Discharge Calendar*, on which motions to discharge committees from further consideration of a bill are placed. A discharge petition must have the support of a majority of the House to be placed on the Discharge Calendar, and discharge motions may only be taken up on the second and fourth Mondays of each month. Few measures reach the floor this way. In the seventy years since the discharge petition was adopted in 1910 only twenty-six out of a total of 909 discharge petitions have been successful.[8] Not only is the requirement of at least 218 signatures to file a discharge petition difficult to obtain, but members are generally unwilling to infringe upon the prerogatives of the committees.

Of the measures on the four legislative calendars, those on the Private Calendar and the Consent Calendar have the easiest route to floor action. Bills on the Private Calendar are called up for consideration on the first Tuesday of each month and, unless two or more members object, are passed without debate. If an objection to the bill is raised by two or more members the bill is referred back to the committee that reported it. Bills on the Consent Calendar are called up for consideration on the first and third Mondays of each month, and are not debated. The first time such a bill is called, a single objection prevents its consideration, and the bill is returned to the Calendar. If a bill is called a second time, three or more objections are required to block it. If a bill is blocked twice it is removed from the Calendar for the remainder of the session.

The procedures used to bring measures on the Private and Consent Calendars to the floor are modified forms of unanimous consent agreements: the opposition of only a very few members is sufficient to prevent the consideration of a measure. Unanimous consent can also be used to bring a measure from any of the other calendars to the floor. One study of the 98th Congress (1983–4) revealed that approximately 34 per cent of the measures considered on the floor were called up through unanimous consent.[9] Another device used to expedite business is the suspension-of-the-rules procedure. By a two-thirds majority vote the House may suspend its normal floor procedures for any bill. The vote to suspend the rules is also a vote to pass the measure: debate is limited to forty minutes and no amendments from the floor may be offered. Such a procedure may only be used on Mondays and Tuesdays, or during the last six days of the session.

The suspension-of-the-rules procedure is normally only used for relatively uncontroversial bills. There was a period during the mid-1970s, however, when Speaker Tip O'Neill used it to expedite the passage of more controversial legislation. In the 95th Congress (1977–8), for example, the House considered 449 bills under suspension-of-the-rules compared with 167 in the 90th Congress (1967–8).[10] This use of the suspension-of-the-rules procedure to expedite business aroused considerable resentment among Republicans, who felt that their minority rights were being infringed, and among some Democrats, who felt that the device denied them the opportunity to give important legislation its due consideration. As a result of this latter disquiet, the Democratic caucus adopted guidelines in 1979 which prohibited any bill with an estimated cost of $100 million in any fiscal year from being processed in this way. Nevertheless, the suspension procedures remain an important method of dealing with legislation. In the 98th Congress, approximately 29 per cent of all measures were dealt with using this device.[11]

The Rules Committee

Although a considerable proportion of the legislation that comes before the House is processed either by consent or by suspension, the normal route to the floor for major bills lies through the Rules Committee.[12] For the first century of its existence, the Rules Committee was a select committee which met at the beginning of each Congress to prepare a biennial set of procedures for the chamber and then went out of existence.[13] In 1880, however, the Rules Committee became a standing committee, and in 1883 it began the practice of issuing special orders or *rules* which if approved by the House, established both the *time* and the *conditions* of debate for individual bills. Despite this development it was not until Speaker Thomas Reed became its chairman that the Rules Committee realized its full potential.[14] Reed turned the committee into an instrument of the Speaker's will. With the other Republicans on the committee, Representative William McKinley (Republican, Ohio) and Joseph Cannon (Republican, Illinois), Reed would determine the details of the rule they wanted for a bill, and then inform the Democratic members of the committee of their decision. 'Gentlemen,' he would tell them, 'we have decided to perpetrate the following outrage.'[15] Essentially, the rule assigns priority to a bill which allows it to take precedence over other bills on the legislative calendar. By granting rules, the Rules Committee performs a vital scheduling function in the House: it allows major bills, which otherwise might not have received floor consideration because of time constraints, to take precedence over minor bills nearer the top of the legislative calendar. As Representative Gillis W. Long (Democrat, Louisiana) stated, the power of the Rules Committee lies in the fact that 'it can sift through legislation coming from the other committees, decide which bills will have right-of-way for consideration on the floor, and determine the order in which legislation will be considered.'[16] Some commentators have likened the Rule Committee's role to that of a 'traffic cop': vital in ensuring a steady flow of legislation to the floor.[17]

The request for a rule is normally made by the chairman of the committee which reported the bill. This request is then considered in much the same manner as legislation is considered in the substantive committees. Hearings are held, and an appropriate rule is agreed by members of the committee. The rule may be *open* and permit any germane amendment to be offered from the floor. It may be *closed* and prohibit the offering of amendments, except those from the committee reporting the bill. Alternatively, a *modified* rule may be granted which permits amendments to some parts of the bill but not to others. A rule might also *waive* points of order against the bill and thus allow the House to violate its own rules when considering the bill. Once a rule has been agreed it is presented to the House for debate and a vote. If a rule is not granted by the Rules Committee the bill is normally considered to be lost, though there are methods of extracting a bill from the committee. Supporters of the bill may try to gain its release from the Rules Committee either through use of a discharge petition, or through what are known as Calendar Wednesday procedures. On Wednesdays, committees may bring up from the House or Union Calendars any measures which have not been granted a rule. The precise regulations governing both of these procedures are very complex, however, and consequently, neither is used very often.[18]

The fact that the Rules Committee is at the centre of the legislative process in the House has meant that the chamber's leadership has usually sought to control its activities.[19] Until 1910 the committee was firmly under the control of the Speaker, who both chaired its meetings and appointed its members. The revolt against the rule of Speaker Joseph Cannon, however, led to the Speaker being removed from the committee, and over the next few decades it began to assert its independence from the leadership. This development reached its peak under the chairmanship of Representative Howard W. Smith (Democrat, Virginia) between 1955 and 1961. With the support of the southern Democrats and Republicans on the committee, Smith not only used delaying tactics to obstruct bills which he opposed, but also forced changes in legislation as a condition for granting a rule. Legislation affected in this way included civil rights bills, aid to education, appropriations measures, statehood for Alaska and Hawaii, housing and aid for depressed areas.[20] By far the most controversial action of the committee, though, occurred in 1960 when the Rules Committee refused to grant a rule allowing the House to agree to a conference with the Senate to resolve differences between the two chambers' versions of a bill giving federal aid to education: an action which killed the bill.[21] In taking this course of action the Committee was apparently placing itself above majority action by both the House and the Senate.

The decision of the Rules Committee not to grant a rule to allow the House to agree to a conference with the Senate led to moves by Speaker Sam Rayburn (Democrat, Texas) to limit the independence of the committee. With the support of a large number of liberals, who had entered the House following the Democratic landslide of 1958, Rayburn won a vote to enlarge the Rules Committee from twelve to fifteen members. The addition of two new Democrats and one new Republican weakened the stranglehold which the conservative coalition had held on the panel, and although Representative Smith remained chairman of the Committee until 1967 he was no longer able to control events as he had done in the past.[22]

Since the early 1970s the Rules Committee has generally been viewed as part of the apparatus of majority party leadership in the House. In part, this development was the result of two institutional changes. First, in an attempt to limit the use of closed rules which prevented the majority from voting for amendments, the Democratic caucus in 1973 adopted a procedure requiring the Democratic members of the Rules Committee to allow a floor vote on any amendment if fifty party members called for a vote and the caucus agreed. Second, the power of the leadership over the Rules Committee

Table 10.1　*Open and restrictive rules, 95th to 99th Congresses*

	Open rules		Closed rules		
	No.	%	No.	%	Total rules
95th　(1977–8)	213	88	28	12	241
96th　(1979–80)	161	81	37	19	198
97th　(1981–2)	90	80	22	20	112
98th　(1983–4)	105	72	40	28	145
99th　(1985–6)	65	64	36	36	101

Note: Closed rules include modified rules and waiver rules.
Source: *Congressional Quarterly Weekly Report*, 10 October 1987, p. 2450.

was strengthened in 1975 when the Democratic caucus authorized the Speaker to appoint, subject to caucus approval, the Democratic members of the committee. Somewhat ironically, however, the leadership has used the Rules Committee to restrict the minority's ability to debate or obstruct legislation. In the ten years after 1977 there was a steady fall in the number of open rules granted to bills (see table 10.1). The use of closed rules to expedite Democratic legislation became even more pronounced when Representative Jim Wright (Democrat, Texas) succeeded Tip O'Neill as Speaker at the beginning of the 100th Congress (1987–8). From the opening of the 100th Congress in January 1987 until 17 September 1987 no fewer than 43 per cent of the bills processed by the Rules Committee were given restricted rules: a fact which led the minority whip Representative Trent Lott (Republican, Mississippi) to complain that: 'The majority leadership is pitching a new shutout at us – shutting out Democrats and Republicans alike.'[23] In fact, Speaker Wright had worked much more closely with the Rules Committee than his predecessor in order to enhance his own power. As Representative Claude Pepper (Democrat, Florida), chairman of the committee since 1983, has stated: 'Wright has acted more upon the assumption that the Rules Committee is a branch of the leadership than Speaker O'Neill did.'[24] Whether Speaker Wright can maintain this tight control remains to be seen.

The Rules Committee is an important centralizing force in an otherwise decentralized chamber. It provides a mechanism for introducing some order into the legislative process. Although the committee can, and occasionally does, act contrary to the wishes of the leadership, it generally works with the Speaker. For this reason, the rules suggested by the committee are rarely rejected on the floor of the House. As Speaker Tip O'Neill once

stated: 'Defeat of the rule on the House floor is considered an af
to the Committee and the Speaker.'[25] Members wishing to challe
may also bear in mind the fact that they might require a rule for their own
bills in the future. Rules are debated for a maximum of one hour and then
voted upon. A majority is required for adoption of the rule.

Debate

After adoption of the rule the House is resolved into the Committee of the
Whole on the State of the Union.[26] This is a parliamentary device which
is used to expedite business, and its procedures differ from those used when
the chamber is operating as the House of Representatives. The Speaker
does not preside, instead he appoints a member of the majority party to
chair the proceedings.[27] A quorum consists of 100 members rather than a
majority of the entire House, and amendments are debated for five minutes
rather than one hour. Finally, debate on sections of the bill may be closed
by unanimous consent or a majority vote of those members present.

The first task of the Committee of the Whole is a general debate on the
measure under consideration. The length of such debate is specified in the
rule granted by the Rules Committee: normally it will be one or two hours,
but occasionally may be much longer. This time is divided equally between
the majority and minority floor managers, who after their initial statements
may invite other members to speak. The task of the majority floor manager
is to gain the passage of the bill while the minority floor manager may
seek to amend or kill it. Normally they will be the chairman and ranking
minority member of the committee which initially reported the bill.

Speeches made during the general discussion of a bill may occasionally
influence the fate of the bill. As Speaker Jim Wright has written: 'Some
votes are always changed by debate.'[28] In general, however, such debates
are largely symbolic: they give credence to the notion that the House arrives
at its decisions in a democratic manner and provide an opportunity for
legislators to take a position to further their chances of re-election. Of more
importance to the final nature of legislation is the amending process.
Provided the bill has not been sent to the floor with a 'closed' or 'modified'
rule, an amendment may be offered by any member. The procedures of
the Committee of the Whole give the amendment's sponsor five minutes to
defend it and an opponent five minutes to attack it. The amendment may
then be brought to a vote. Amendments may be offered either as a serious
attempt to change the substantive content of a bill, or else as a dilatory
tactic. As each amendment must be read out and debated for at least five
minutes, the tactic of offering up numerous amendments can be used to
obstruct the passage of the legislation under consideration.

Voting

After all amendments have been voted upon, the Committee of the Whole 'rises' and the chamber is reconstituted as the House of Representatives with the Speaker in the chair. The purpose of the House is to ratify the decisions taken in the Committee of the Whole. No further debate or amendment is possible, but the Speaker will ask if any representative wishes to have a separate vote on any of the bill's amendments before the bill as a whole is put to the vote. If no separate vote is requested the changes made in the Committee of the Whole are deemed to have been approved. A minority party member who opposes the bill will then ask for it to be recommitted to the committee which reported it; effectively killing the bill if successful. Following the defeat of the recommital motion the Speaker will ask the House to vote on the entire bill.

There are five methods of voting in the House of Representatives: a voice vote, when the Speaker judges from the volume of shouts of aye or nay that answer him which side is in the majority; a division, when members stand and are counted; a teller vote, when tellers are appointed for each side, and those supporting or opposing the measure pass by their respective tellers; a 'teller with clerks' vote in which the names of those passing by each teller are recorded; and a yea and nay vote, when the clerk reads out the name of each member who answers Yea or Nay. When a vote has been taken by one method, a different kind of vote can be requested at any time before the result of the first vote has been announced. After the result of the vote on the bill has been announced, a *pro forma* motion to reconsider is made, and normally tabled, or postponed indefinitely, to prevent the bill from being reconsidered later. This is because the rules of the House state that a final vote is only conclusive if there has been an opportunity to reconsider it on the same or following day.

Rule by the Majority

From this description it can be seen that the floor procedures of the House of Representatives have been structured to facilitate rule by the majority. As long as the Rules Committee is under the control of the leadership there is little opportunity for the minority to obstruct the wishes of the majority for any great period of time. This is not the case in the Senate where an obdurate minority may frustrate the wishes of the majority almost at will.

THE US SENATE

Although the Senate has a complex set of rules to guide both its scheduling and consideration of legislation, in practice its procedures are far more flexible than those of the House of Representatives. The small size of the chamber, its constitutional design as a guardian of the rights of the states and the various pressures acting upon its members, have usually meant that the greatest possible consideration is given to individual needs when dealing with legislation. All senators have an opportunity to participate in the scheduling of business, minor bills are usually dealt with very quickly to save time for more controversial measures and the formal rules are often suspended by unanimous consent agreements.[29]

The Scheduling of Business

As in the House, the first stage in the process for obtaining floor action in the Senate for a measure reported out of a committee is for it to be placed on a calendar. Unlike the House, however, the Senate has only two calendars: all legislation is placed on the *Calendar of General Orders*; treaties and executive nominations are placed on the *Executive Calendar*. Any senator may propose a motion to call up a measure on either calendar. If this motion is made during the first two hours of a session, known as the 'morning hour', it is not debatable. Otherwise the motion may be subject to a debate and a possible filibuster. Occasionally, a controversial bill may be defeated at this stage. A more common technique for scheduling business is through unanimous consent agreements. Both minor and major bills may be brought to the floor in this way. Typically, minor bills may be called up and passed without debate. As a single objection means a unanimous consent agreement is not possible, the leaders of both parties are careful to check with senators to ensure that there are no objections before the bill is brought to the floor. In this way minor bills may be passed in a matter of minutes. Unanimous consent agreements for major bills will normally place a limit on debate, will occasionally restrict the amending process and will specify the time for a final vote on the measure.

To a certain extent the Senate's unanimous consent agreements may be viewed as the functional equivalent of the rules granted by the Rules Committee in the House. Both waive the rules of their respective chambers. Both must be approved by the membership of their respective chambers: in the Senate by unanimous consent, and in the House by majority vote. Finally, both provide a means for the party leadership to play a role in the scheduling of legislation. The main difference between the two devices is the fact that unanimous consent agreements are worked out in private between individuals, while rules are drafted in public by a standing committee.

The Amending Process

When a bill reaches the floor of the Senate it becomes subject to almost unlimited amendment unless a unanimous consent agreement specifies otherwise.[30] Moreover, except in the cases of general appropriations bills, concurrent budget resolutions, bills on which cloture has been invoked and measures regulated by unanimous consent agreements, such amendments need not be germane.[31]'Amendments may be made so as totally to alter the nature of the proposition' wrote Thomas Jefferson in the parliamentary manual he prepared during his service as president of the Senate (1797–1801).[32] Non-germane amendments, or riders, are in fact a very potent legislative weapon in certain circumstances. As the President of the United States is empowered to veto bills in their entirety only, and does not possess an 'item veto', riders have often been used to by-pass presidential opposition to a measure. They have also been used to by-pass unsympathetic committees in the Senate. In 1960, for example, Majority Leader Senator Lyndon B. Johnson (Democrat, Texas) circumvented a hostile Judiciary Committee by offering a civil rights bill as an amendment to a measure providing aid to a school district in Missouri. Similarly, if a bill gets stuck in a committee it may be offered as an amendment to an unrelated bill from the floor. In this sense, the use of riders allows individual senators to discharge bills from committees. Finally, non-germane amendments may be used to advance the agendas of special interest groups. The most blatant example of this type of action is the introduction of what has become known as a 'Christmas Tree Bill' at the end of almost every congressional session. A Christmas Tree Bill is usually a minor measure which has been passed by the House to which the Senate has attached a wide variety of non-germane amendments catering to the wishes of special interests.

The relative openness of the Senate's amending process has recently been the subject of much debate. Its supporters argue that the practice allows the chamber to respond quickly to changes in public opinion and offers a chance to overturn any arbitrary action taken by the committees. On the other hand, its opponents point out that the technique is often used to obstruct legislation. If a bill becomes laden with controversial amendments it may well fail to gain acceptance. The tradition of an unlimited amending process is also a time-consuming practice: amendments have to be read and voted upon. Accepting the need for change, the Temporary Select Committee to Study the Senate's Committee System, chaired by Senator Dan Quayle (Republican, Indiana), suggested in 1984 that a non-germane amendment require sixty votes before being accepted.[33] The suggestion, however, was not acted upon. Another attempt to tighten the amending process was made in 1986 when a provision requiring amendments to be germane if agreed by two-thirds of the Senate's membership was included in the resolution establishing television coverage of the chamber's debates (Senate Resolution 28). [34] Again this provision was defeated.

The Filibuster

Attempts to limit the flexibility of the Senate's amending process have generally failed because the tradition reflects the deference accorded to individual senators as the ambassadors of their states. This deference also lies behind the chamber's tradition of unlimited debate which originally developed out of the norms of courtesy and respect afforded to each senator.[35] Although important in all legislatures, it is only in the Senate that the ability to delay legislation, or filibuster, by refusing to end debate has remained practically unhindered.[36] The Senate provided the means to invoke cloture, or cut off debate, in 1917 with the adoption of Rule 22 following a particularly controversial filibuster against a proposal by President Woodrow Wilson to arm US merchant ships in order to give them some protection against German submarines. In general, however, efforts to ease the requirements for cloture have been resisted. From 1917 to 1975 Rule 22 provided that debate could only be closed by a two-thirds majority vote. For most of this period this meant two-thirds of the senators present and voting, but between 1949 and 1959 the rule was strengthened to require a two-thirds vote of the entire Senate membership. In 1975, following a decade of accusations by liberal Democrats that the policy preferences of the majority party were being obstructed by a small minority, the rule was relaxed with the passage of Senate Resolution 4 (1975). This rule change reduced the vote needed to approve a cloture motion to a three-fifths majority of the Senate's membership.

During the debate over Senate Resolution 4 (1975) the Majority Leader, Senator Mike Mansfield (Democrat, Montana), indicated just how important the tradition of extended debate was to the Senate when he expressed his fears that the proposed changes in Rule 22 would: 'destroy . . . the very uniqueness of this body; to relegate it to the status of any other legislative body and to diminish the Senate as an institution of this government'.[37] In other words, the right to extended debate is regarded as a unique characteristic of the Senate. It is initimately bound up with the role of senators as ambassadors from their states, with the notion of the protection of minority rights and is generally thought to be something worth protecting.

Ironically, the relaxation in the requirements necessary to invoke cloture in 1975 coincided with an increase in the frequency of filibusters. Previously, the filibuster had been used almost exclusively in the debates on the great issues of the day. Senator Huey Long (Democrat, Louisiana), for example, carried out a fifteen hour filibuster in 1935 against a proposal to modify the National Recovery Act of 1933. During the course of this speech Senator Long spoke on a wide range of subjects, at one stage informing his colleagues on how to fry oysters and prepare potlikker. When he noticed that many senators were dozing in their seats he suggested that they should be compelled to listen to him unless excused. Vice-President Garner, who was presiding over the Senate, replied that: 'That would be unusual cruelty under the Bill of Rights.'[38] Most commonly the filibuster was used by southern Democrats opposed to civil rights legislation. Indeed, Senator Strom Thurmond (Democrat, South Carolina) set the record for an individual filibuster when he spoke for twenty-four hours and eighteen minutes against the Civil Rights Bill of 1957.[39] Before beginning his filibuster Senator Thurmond spent two days drying out in the Senate's steam room so that toilet calls would not force him to surrender the floor. Since the mid-1970s, however, filibusters hav been waged over issues of a more transient nature than the New Deal or segregation. In part this is due to generational changes in the Senate's membership: many of the senators gaining election in this period were young, politically inexperienced and unwilling to compromise on issues.[40] Also important, though, was the 1975 change to Rule 22 which, by making it easier to end filibusters, made their use more frequent.

Some indication of the increase in the use of filibusters can be gained by noting the increase in the number of cloture votes over the past decade. Of the 245 cloture votes between 1917 and September 1987, no fewer than 58 per cent occurred after 1975. With the threat of a filibuster more likely it is now routine to file a cloture motion, which requires sixteen signatures, as soon as a bill is sent to the floor for consideration. Remarking on this development Senator Quayle suggested that: 'The Senate has cloturitis. We invoke it here, there, and everywhere.'[41]

In addition to a general broadening in the type of legislative measures liable to be filibustered, the late 1970s also saw the development of the post-cloture filibuster by Senator James Allen (Democrat, Alabama). Under the guidance of his mentor, Senator Richard B. Russell (Democrat, Georgia), Senator Allen studied the Senate's rules carefully enough to discover that all was not lost when cloture was invoked. Dilatory motions and amendments, together with roll call votes and quorum calls, could still delay the passage of a bill for days. Such tactics, which were strongly reminiscent of the methods used in the House of Representatives during the speakership of Thomas B. Reed, were first used by Senator Allen in 1976, during the

Senate's consideration of an anti-trust enforcement bill, when he broke the convention that a filibuster ended when cloture was invoked. He charged that the leadership had cut him off before he had actually begun to filibuster, and in doing so had violated his minority rights. He argued that: 'we have a steamroller rolling in the Senate, and I do not appreciate it, for one.'[42] In retaliation he called up dozens of amendments, and demanded quorum calls and roll call votes after cloture had been invoked, and did not relent until he had been offered a compromise.

The same tactics were used with considerable success in 1977 by two maverick Democrats who were determined to kill legislation designed to end price controls on natural gas. Senators James Abourezk (Democrat, South Dakota) and Howard Metzenbaum (Democrat, Ohio) launched a standard filibuster, and when cloture was invoked tried to amend the bill to death. The two senators had filed 508 amendments before cloture, and they began to call them up for consideration. They insisted that the clerk of the Senate read the amendments, and repeatedly demanded roll call votes and quorum calls.

The Abourezk-Metzenbaum post-cloture filibuster was eventually ended in dramatic fashion when Vice-President Walter Mondale, with the cooperation of Majority Leader Senator Robert Byrd (Democrat, West Virginia) and Minority Leader Senator Howard Baker (Republican, Tennessee), ruled the amendments to be out of order and, therefore, not pending business before the Senate.[43] In an attempt to restrict the use of the post-cloture filibuster, a change in Rule 22 was made in 1979. After cloture had been invoked a final vote had to occur after 100 hours of further debate. All quorum calls and votes were included in the 100 hours, but provision was made to extend the time for debate if approved by a two-thirds majority vote. In 1986, a new limit of thirty hours of post-cloture debate was introduced as part of the package providing for the televising of Senate debates. Despite these attempts to reduce the opportunities for post-cloture obstruction, delaying tactics of this sort are still frequently used in the Senate. In February 1988, for example, the Republicans sought to filibuster a bill which proposed to introduce new campaign spending limits by asking for quorum calls and then boycotting the votes. Should the Democrats have been unable to find fifty-one votes to make the quorum, then the Senate would have had to adjourn. Finally becoming exasperated by these tactics, Senator Byrd took advantage of a clause contained in Article I, Section 5 of the Constitution, which enabled each House 'to compel the attendance of absent members, in such a manner, and under such penalties, as each House shall provide', and ordered the Senate's sergeant-at-arms to arrest absent senators and bring them to the floor. Eventually, Senator Bob Packwood (Republican, Oregon) was arrested and carried to the floor of the Senate to make up a quorum. Such strong-arm tactics by the leadership predictably led to many complaints from Republicans. Senator Arlen Specter (Republican, Pennsylvania) complained of the 'tyranny of the majority leader', while his colleague, Senator Orrin Hatch (Republican, Utah) suggested that the Democrats were trying to turn the Senate into a 'banana republic'.[44]

Although the conditions necessary to invoke cloture were eased in 1975, and the opportunities to launch post-cloture filibusters limited by the rule changes of 1979 and 1986, obstructionist techniques on the floor of the Senate can still delay the passage of legislation. In an attempt to ensure that a filibuster against a controversial bill does not bring the entire business of the Senate to a halt, majority leaders since the early 1970s have used what is known as 'the track system'. This system allows the Senate to have several pieces of legislation pending on the floor at the same time by specifying different periods of the day when each proposal is to be considered.[45] It means, as Senator Alan Cranston (Democrat, California) explained, that the Senate 'can . . . continue to work on all other legislation on one "track" while a filibuster against a particular piece of legislation is . . . in progress on the other "track"'.[46] The use of the track system is implemented by the majority Leader after obtaining the unanimous consent of the chamber.

Voting

A final vote on a bill occurs whenever the floor debate comes to a close. Voting can either be by voice, when the volume of support for a measure is gauged; by division, when senators stand to be counted; or by roll call, when each senator's vote is recorded.[47] Following a vote by one method, a different kind of vote can be requested at any time before the result of the first vote has been announced. Any senator who voted for the winning side, or who did not vote, can request the matter to be reconsidered in another vote within the next two days. As a vote may be reconsidered only once, and to lessen the chances of defections, it is usual for a member of the winning side to offer a motion to reconsider immediately after the first vote. In practice, a further motion to 'table', and thus effectively kill, the motion to reconsider is then made. A motion to table is not subject to debate, and if successful disposes of the motion to reconsider.

Rule by the Individual

From this description it can be seen that there are considerable differences between the floor procedures of the Senate and the House of Representatives. The larger, more complex, House operates on the basis of the formal vote which allows the majority to dominate. The Senate, on the other hand, tends to use informal arrangements which accommodate the interests of the individual. Far greater leeway is given to the senator than to the representative when scheduling business, offering amendments and in debate. This emphasis on individual rights makes it much more difficult to construct winning coalitions in the Senate than in the House. Legislative coalitions must be painstakingly negotiated, and constantly subject to revision, in order to minimize the likelihood of obstruction. Only by taking account of the wishes of most of its members will legislation pass through the Senate.

THE CONFERENCE COMMITTEE

Before a bill can be presented to the President for his signature or veto any differences in the versions passed by the House and the Senate must be reconciled. Often this can be done fairly easily. Either one chamber can simply adopt the other's version of a bill, or else the two chambers may send the bill back and forth between them, amending each other's amendments until identical language is arrived at. For approximately 25 per cent of all public bills, however, the differences between the House and Senate are resolved in a conference committee composed of members of each chamber. This role means that the conference committee occupies an extremely important position in the legislative process. As Representative Dennis E. Eckart (Democrat, Ohio) has stated: 'Conference Committees are the ultimate high for legislators. They are the Supreme Court of legislation. If you don't get it here, there's no other place to go.'[48]

Although the Constitution does not mention conference committees as an instrument for resolving bicameral differences, their use in Congress was assured when on the first day of the First Congress the Senate appointed a committee to prepare rules for conferences. During the First Congress conferences were used to deal with measures such as the Bill of Rights, the salaries of members, the Treasury Bill, the Post Office Bill and a bill regulating the courts. Over the next fifty years, the use of the conference committee as a legislative institution became firmly established as the need for some mechanism to break the recurring deadlock between a mutually hostile House and Senate in the period before the Civil War became apparent. By 1852 the essential elements of the modern conference system had evolved.[49]

A conference committee for a bill is established when both the House and the Senate formally vote to disagree with the other chamber's bill. Once agreement to establish a conference committee has been obtained, the Speaker of the House, and the presiding officer of the Senate, select the conferees. In practice, the Speaker and presiding officer defer to the chairman and ranking minority member of the committee having jurisdiction over the legislation when making their appointments. Prior to the procedural reforms of the 1970s, seniority tended to be the main criterion in the choice of conferees. The general challenge to seniority in both chambers, however, has meant that members are now chosen who possess a particular interest or expertise in the subject of the bill. Increasingly, this has resulted in members of the subcommittees which reported the bill being appointed as conferees. There is no limit on the size of each chamber's delegation to the conference committee. As each chamber has one vote in conference, determined by a majority of its conferees, numerical differences in the sizes of the delegations from the House and Senate are unimportant. Interestingly, one recent trend has been for conference delegations to become larger. This is the result both of the increasing complexity of legislation, and the demands of junior members to have access to this important stage in the legislative process. On the 1981 omnibus Budget Reconciliation Bill, for example, there were 250 conferees working in fifty-eight subconferences. The second largest conference cocurred in 1986 when there were 242 conferees working in thirty-one subconferences on that year's omnibus Budget Reconciliation Bill. Whatever the size of each chamber's delegation, a majority must be from the majority party in the chamber. In general, party ratios in the delegation reflect party ratios in the parent chamber.

The bargaining which takes place within the conference committee is, perhaps, the most difficult in the entire legislative process. Both sides need to search for a compromise solution which will be acceptable to their chambers. If no agreement can be reached the measure dies at this stage. Until 1975 conference committees were usually held in secret.[50] In 1975 both chambers adopted rules, as part of the general movement to bring 'government into the sunshine', requiring open meetings unless the conferees voted in public session to close the meeting. In 1977, the House adopted a further rule which required open conference meetings unless the full chamber agreed to a closed session. As with the rule changes requiring open committee hearings and mark-ups, the net effect of the sunshine rules has been to provide interest groups with a further opportunity to observe the actions of members of Congress. Some have argued that this has led to greater difficulty in arriving at compromise positions. Whereas previously a member might have been willing to drop a particular amendment, under the gaze of the lobbyists they are more likely to fight for its retention. Particularly if the issue could be used against them in an election campaign.[51]

When the majority of the conferees from each chamber have reached agreement, the compromise bill is written as a report. This report is then presented to each chamber for a final vote. Both chambers require conference reports to be accepted or rejected in their entirety. In the Senate the report may be filibustered. If there are any amendments upon which the conference has been unable to agree, known officially as 'amendments in disagreement', then a separate vote will be taken. As with the main bill, all amendments must pass in identical language through both chambers to be acceptable. In general, conference reports are seldom rejected. To do so would not only kill the legislation, but would also display a lack of deference towards the conference committee. Once the conference report is accepted by both chambers, a copy of the bill is enrolled by a clerk, and then signed by the Speaker of the House and the presiding officer of the Senate. It is then sent to the President for his approval or veto.

Although the floor procedures in the Senate tend to stress individual rights, and those in the House tend to support rule by the majority, the legislative process as a whole is remarkable for its openness. Individuals and groups have access to the decision-making process, and individual senators and representatives may have a real impact on policy. While such a system stresses the 'democratic' nature of Congress, it does mean that policy is difficult to enact. To be passed into law a measure needs to overcome a number of obstacles. In recent years the increased importance of constituency concerns has made these obstacles even more formidable as political power has become fragmented. Overcoming such fragmentation and ensuring that the institution functions is the role of the party leaders in both chambers.

Notes

1 The House provided for the televised coverage of its debates in 1978; the Senate followed suit in 1986.

2 See Kenneth Bradshaw and David Pring *Parliament and Congress* (London, Quartet, 1981), p. 141.

3 Quoted in DeAlva Stanwood Alexander *History and Procedure of the House of Representatives* (Boston, Houghton Mifflin, 1916), p. 187.

4 Quoted in Samuel W. McCall *The Life of Thomas Beckett Reed* (Boston, Houghton Mifflin, 1914), pp. 167–8.

5 Quoted in Hubert Bruce Fuller *The Speaker of the House* (Boston, Little, Brown, 1909), pp. 222–3.

6 Cited in *Congressional Quarterly Weekly Report*, 3 January 1987, p. 35.

7 *Congressional Quarterly Weekly Report*, 12 March 1988, p. 671.

8 *How Congress Works* (Washington DC, Congressional Quarterly Press, 1983), p. 56.

9 See Roger H. Davidson and Walter J. Oleszek *Congress and its Members* (Washington DC, Congressional Quarterly Press, 1985), p. 271.

10 *How Congress Works*, p. 55.

11 Davidson and Oleszek *Congress and its Members*, p. 271.

12 Six committees have direct access to the floor for selective bills: Appropriations, Budget, House Administration, Rules, Standards of Official Conduct and Ways and Means. Even these committees will normally seek a rule to protect their bills from amendments or points of order.

13 The Rules Committee was established in April 1789 to draw up rules for the First Congress.

14 Neil MacNeil *Forge of Democracy* (New York, David McKay, 1963), p. 53.

15 George Rothwell Brown *The Leadership of Congress* (Indianapolis, Bobbs-Merrill, 1922), p. 88.

16 Gillis W. Long quoted in Walter J. Oleszek *Congressional Procedures and the Policy Process* (Washington DC, Congressional Quarterly Press, 1984), p. 104.

17 See Spark M. Matsanuga and Ping Chen *Rulemakers of the House* (Chicago, University of Illinois Press, 1976), pp. 20–5.

18 See Oleszek *Congressional Procedures*, pp. 117–20.

19 The Speaker became chairman of the Rules Committee in 1859 when it was still technically a select committee.

20 See Charles O. Jones 'Joseph G. Cannon and Howard W. Smith: An Essay on the Limits of Leadership in the House of Representatives' in Matthew D. McCubbins and Terry Sullivan eds *Congress: Structure and Policy* (Cambridge, Cambridge University Press, 1987), p. 275.

21 Ibid. p. 276.

22 See James A. Robinson *The House Rules Committee* (Indianapolis, Bobbs-Merrill, 1963); and Robert L. Peabody 'The Enlarged Rules Committee' in Robert L. Peabody and Nelson W. Polsby eds *New Perspectives on the House of Representatives* (Chicago, Rand McNally, 1969).

23 *Congressional Quarterly Weekly Report*, 10 October 1987, p. 2450.

24 Ibid. p. 2451.

25 *Congressional Quarterly Weekly Report*, 14 February 1976, p. 313.

26 Technically, only bills on the Union Calendar must be considered in the Committee of the Whole. In practice, most major bills are considered in this way.

27 This practice dates back to English parliamentary procedure. Historically, the Speaker of the House of Commons was regarded as an agent of the Crown. The artifact of the Committee of the Whole was designed so that the Commons could elect their own chairman and discuss matters relating to the Crown without the normal restrictions of a House of Commons session.

28 Jim Wright *You and Your Congressman* (New York, Coward-McCann, 1965), p. 153.

29 The interesting question of why unanimous consent agreements should be so common in such an individualistic body as the US Senate is discussed in Keith Krehbiel 'Unanimous Consent Agreements: Getting Along in the Senate' *Journal of Politics* (August), 1986, pp. 541–64.

30 Much of the material on amending and filibustering in the Senate is to be found in Christopher J. Bailey *The Republican Party in the US Senate 1974–1984* (Manchester, Manchester University Press, 1988), ch. 2.

31 See Stanley Bach 'Germaneness Rules and Bicameral Relations in the US Congress' *Legislative Studies Quarterly* (August), 1982, pp. 341–57.

32 *Constitution, Jefferson: Manual and Rules of the House of Representatives* 97th Congress, 2nd sess. H. Doc. 97–271 p. 235.

33 *Congressional Quarterly Weekly Report*, 1 December 1984, p. 3035.

34 *Congressional Quarterly Weekly Report*, 1 March 1986, p. 520.

35 See Richard R. Beeman 'Unlimited Debate in the Senate: The First Phrase' *Political Science Quarterly* (September), 1968, pp. 419–59.

36 For a history of the filibuster see Franklin L. Burdette *Filibustering in the Senate* (Princeton, Princeton University Press, 1940).

37 *Congressional Quarterly Weekly Report*, 22 February 1975, p. 412.

38 For an account of this episode see T. Harry Williams *Huey Long* (New York, Bantam, 1969), pp. 874–7.

39 Senator Thurmond became a Republican in 1964.

40 See Christopher J. Bailey 'The US Senate: The New Individualism and the New Right' *Parliamentary Affairs* (July), 1986, pp. 354–67.

41 *Congressional Record* 98th Congress, 2nd sess., 28 September 1984, p. S12271.

42 *Congressional Quarterly Weekly Report*, 1 March 1976, p. 460.

43 For an account of this episode see Howard H. Baker *No Margin for Error* (New York, Times Books, 1980), pp. 30–2.

44 *Congressional Quarterly Weekly Report*, 27 March 1988, p. 487.

45 Oleszek *Congressional Procedures*, pp. 157–8.

46 *Congressional Record* 94th Congress, 21 January 1975, p. S928.

47 Bradshaw and Pring *Parliament and Congress*, p. 202.

48 *Congressional Quarterly Weekly Report*, 6 September 1986, p. 2080.

49 By far the most comprehensive study of the development of the conference committee is Ada C. McCown *The Congressional Conference Committee* (New York, Columbia University Press, 1927). Another important study is David J. Vogler *The Third House* (Evanston, Northwestern University Press, 1971).

50 The very first conference committee in 1789 was held in open session. The next open conference was not until 1911. Since 1975 most conferences have been open.

51 Davidson and Oleszek *Congress and its Members*, p. 284.

11

Leadership

Although the Constitution makes only scant reference to the role of leaders in Congress, and does not mention political parties at all, the party leaders have, in fact, become one of the most important factors influencing the way in which the House and the Senate function. The firm establishment of the two-party system in Congress in the period following the Civil War has encouraged congressional leaders to develop practices which further their party's effectiveness. They have sought to promote party unity, manipulate the rules to serve their party's or the President's legislative goals and improve their party's electoral fortunes by enhancing its national image. Essentially, this means ensuring that the institution functions efficiently so that party objectives may be pursued. The role of the party leaders is to provide a centralizing force in an institution where the emphasis is upon fragmentation.

The degree of success which the leaders have enjoyed in performing their functions has varied considerably. To understand why this should be the case it is necessary to recognize that the leadership structure, like the committee system, has developed to meet the demands of the institution's membership. Individual members have granted authority to the leadership only because by so doing they serve their own interests. This means that the authority of the leadership is acutely sensitive to the changing goals of representatives and senators. If these goals require strong *party* performance then the position of the leadership will be strengthened; if, on the other hand, they require a demonstration of *independence* then the position of the leadership will be weakened. Analysing the role of the leadership is a useful means, therefore, not only of furthering a knowledge of the way Congress works but it also provides an illustration of the way in which changing membership goals affect institutional arrangements.

THE HOUSE OF REPRESENTATIVES

The Speaker

The Speaker, the majority and minority leaders, and the majority and minority whips, are the fundamental components of the party leadership structure in the contemporary House of Representatives. Of these five offices, by far the most important is that of the Speaker. It is the only one mentioned in the Constitution. Article I, Section 2 states that: 'The House of Representatives shall choose their speaker and other Officers.' The Speakership is also the only office mentioned in the Rules of the House. These factors mean that the Speaker enjoys a visibility and authority which is unsurpassed by any other member of Congress, either in the House or the Senate.

Whether the Founding Fathers intended the Speaker to become the central figure in the House's leadership structure is a matter of debate. The Constitutional Convention of 1787 did not debate the nature of the office, nor is the post mentioned in the *Federalist Papers*. The antipathy felt by most of the Founding Fathers towards the idea of political parties suggests that they did not intend the Speaker to become a *party* leader. In *Federalist* (1), for example, Alexander Hamilton gave vent to this anti-party sentiment when he declared: 'nothing could be more ill-judged than that intolerant spirit, which has, at all times, characterized political parties.'[1] On the other hand, there is evidence to suggest that the Founding Fathers did intend the Speaker to be a *political* leader and not merely an impartial umpire of parliamentary battles.[2] Not only did most of the colonial legislatures have Speakers who used their positions to advance legislative programmes, but one proposal put before the Constitutional Convention of 1787 called for the establishment of a Council of State composed of the Speaker, the President, the president of the Senate (the Vice-President), the Chief Justice, and the heads of the departments. Although rejected by the Convention, the fact that the Speaker was to be included in a Council of State suggests that his role was conceived as more than just that of a parliamentarian. If this is indeed the case then it would be a mistake to equate the speakership of the House of Representatives with that of the British House of Commons. The latter is a non-partisan presiding officer, and not a political leader.[3]

Rules adopted during the First Congress (1789–91) gave the Speaker powers which reflected the parliamentary and political functions expected of the Office. The Speaker was given the right to preside over sessions of the House, to put questions to the House, to decide points of order, to announce the results of votes, to appoint the members of select committees and to make a 'casting' vote in cases of a tie. Together, these rights constituted a source of considerable *potential* authority. As one distingished nineteenth-century scholar noted: 'The Speakership is not only an institution, it is an opportunity, in which men of strong character have shown their leadership . . . The degree of influence which any individual Speaker attains depends as much upon the man as the office.'[4] It was by using their right to preside over debates, to decide on points of order and to appoint members to committees that Speakers such as Henry Clay (1811–20, 1823–5), Thomas Reed (1889–91, 1895–9) and Joseph Cannon (1903–10) managed to exercise almost absolute control over the activities of the House.

The fact that the political parties had not emerged by the First Congress meant that the first Speaker, Frederick A. Muhlenberg of Pennsylvania, was able to act simply as a presiding officer. As the political parties began to coalesce over the next two decades, however, so Speakers became more partisan figures.[5] This development was confirmed with the election of Henry Clay (Democratic-Republican, Kentucky) as Speaker in November 1811 on his first day in the House.[6] Clay owed his election to the support of a group of Democratic-Republicans, known as the War Hawks, who favoured western expansion and war with England. To promote the legislative agenda of this group Clay used the latent powers of the Speaker to assert his authority over the activities of the House. He appointed War Hawks to the Foreign Affairs, Military Affairs and Naval Affairs Committees in order to engender committee reports recommending war against England, and used his powers as presiding officer to refuse recognition to members wishing to speak in debate against war. So effective were his efforts that on 15 March 1812 he was able to present President Madison with a proposal calling for a declaration of war.

There is little doubt that Henry Clay should be viewed as the first great Speaker of the House of Representatives. His activities strengthened the parliamentary powers of the office, enhanced the personal authority of the Speaker over the chamber and elevated Clay to a position where he rivalled President Madison in terms of prestige and fame, if not power.[7] In other words, Clay was responsible for firmly establishing the political role of the speakership. By his actions he ensured that the Speaker would not be viewed as an impartial parliamentarian but as the legislative leader of the majority party.

Although Clay was clearly a leader of his party, and his model of the speakership was followed by most of his pre-Civil War successors, the first Speaker to use the party organization and enforce party discipline in a systematic way to support his leadership was James G. Blaine (Republican, Maine). Elected Speaker in 1869 Blaine declared that as he had been 'chosen by the party representing the political majority in the House' he owed 'a faithful allegiance to the principles and policy of that party'.[8] By using his powers of patronage Blaine was able to control the House and make it responsive to the will of the Republican party.[9] The result was a torrent of legislation favourable to business interests.

One of Speaker Blaine's most important innovations was to use the party caucus to force agreement on the party's candidate for Speaker. Thus although the Speaker was formally chosen by a roll call vote of the House, in practice, he is selected by a secret ballot of the majority party.[10] This development, together with the fact that the Speaker was emerging as a leading party figure, meant that the pattern of recruitment to the office began to change. Whereas previously it had been possible for an individual to be elected as Speaker after only a few years service in the House, the evolution of the office as an important party position meant that the speakership increasingly came to be filled with more senior legislators. In the period between 1861 and 1910 the number of years served in the House by Speakers prior to their election was 10.8 years compared with a mere 6.3 years between 1789 and 1861. During the twentieth century this trend has become even more pronounced. Between 1910 and 1988 Speakers had served an average of 25.1 years in the House before gaining election. It is also normal practice, particularly among Democrats, for them to have worked their way up through the party organization, serving first as whip, then as floor leader, before gaining election as Speaker.

James Blaine's tenure as Speaker marked the beginning of four decades of almost unchecked growth in the power of the speakership. Speakers Samuel J. Randall (1876–81), John G. Carlisle (1883–9), Thomas B. Reed, Charles F. Crisp (1891–5) and Joseph G. Cannon not only extended the use of the office's existing powers of appointment, recognition and points of order, but also used their position as chairmen of the newly revitalized Rules Committee to control the flow of legislation to the floor. Speaker Cannon, in particular, used his powers to impose his will on the House in a manner which earned him the epithet of 'czar'. Some indication of the extent of Cannon's power can be seen by the fact that one representative, when asked by a constituent for a copy of the House's rules and regulations, merely sent a picture of the Speaker.[11]

Speaker Cannon was gradually stripped of much of his power between 1909 and 1910. In 1909 the House created a Consent Calendar to provide for the routine consideration of unopposed bills, and established the Calendar Wednesday and Discharge Petition procedures to provide means to expedite business blocked by the leadership.[12] On 19 March 1910 the Speaker was removed from the Rules Committee after a bitter floor debate. In 1911 a further aspect of the Speaker's power was removed when the House changed its rules to provide for the election by the full House of all standing committees and their chairmen. The result of these changes was the weakening of the party leadership in the House as power flowed to the committee chairmen. It was not until 1975 that a successful attempt to restore some of the Speaker's former powers was made. In that year, the Democratic caucus agreed to make the Speaker the chairman of the party's Steering and Policy Committees, the group which determines Democratic committee assignments. The caucus also agreed to allow the Speaker to nominate all members of the Rules Committee and choose its chairman.

The revolt against Speaker Cannon was important, not only because it helped to shape the modern office, but also because it shows that no matter how powerful a leader in Congress may appear to be he has never been able to thwart the wishes of the majority for any significant period of time.[13] Cannon's power was predicated upon the unusual levels of party homogeneity existing at this time, and the domination of the party machines which ensured the selection of legislators who were used to acquiescing to the wishes of those in authority. As these factors changed so the basis of Cannon's power crumbled away. New patterns of electoral competition reduced the homogeneity of the parties, and Progressive reforms weakened the role of the machines in the selection of candidates. The result was a new generation of legislators unwilling to defer to Cannon's leadership.

Perhaps the most significant point to emerge from a study of the development of the speakership is that although individuals gifted with certain political skills may shape the office to a certain extent, it is the overall institutional environment which is by far the most important determinant of leadership power in the House.[14] Acknowledgement of this fact is essential in order to understand the position of the Speaker in the contemporary House. Although the 1975 rule changes increased the resources available to the Speaker, other reforms have strengthened the prerogatives of individual members. The problem for modern Speakers, therefore, is to use their resources effectively within an environment which is both unpredictable and highly individualistic.[15] It is a problem which most Speakers have attempted to solve by expanding the number of members within the leadership's ranks, and providing services of use to individuals. Figure 11.1 shows the leadership structure of the House of Representatives in the 100th Congress.

Floor Leaders

The initial development of an expanded leadership structure in the House can be traced back to 1899, when Speaker David B. Henderson (Republican, Iowa) appointed Representative Sereno Payne (Republican, New York) as the first officially designated majority leader.[16] In 1911, when the Democrats

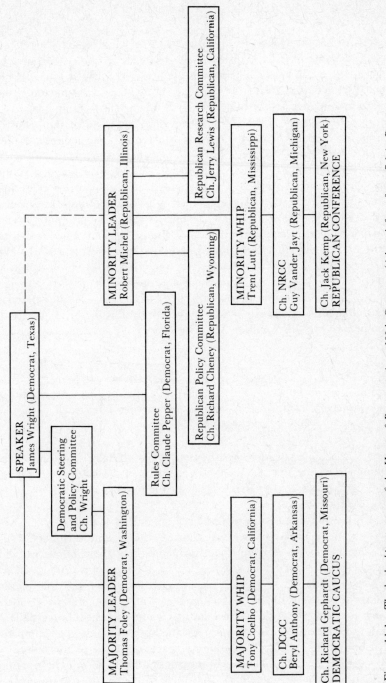

Figure 11.1 *The leadership structure of the House of Representatives, 100th Congress. (Adapted from figure 7.1 in Roger H. Davidson and Walter J. Oleszek Congress and its Members (Washington DC, Congressional Quarterly Press, 1985), p. 172)*

gained control of the House, Representative Oscar Underwood (Democrat, Alabama) became the first majority leader to be elected by secret ballot of the party caucus.[17] The position of minority leader first became identifiable in 1883.[18] Since that time the post has always been assumed by the candidate nominated by the minority party for the speakership.

House and party rules are silent concerning the duties of the majority and minority leaders. From 1925 onwards, however, the majority leader has been viewed as the Speaker's principal lieutenant. This point was made by Majority Leader Jim Wright (Democrat, Texas) who noted that the majority leader 'must work *with* the Speaker, in a supportive role, and never against him'.[19] The task of the majority leader is to help the Speaker and other party leaders to formulate the party's legislative programme, and then guide that programme through the House. He must negotiate with committee chairmen to ensure that important bills are reported by the committees, and then consult with party members in order to schedule floor action. The key words here are *negotiate* and *consult*. Except through the Speaker, the majority leader has no power to use the rules of the House to attain legislative goals. His power is derived from being at the centre of communications in the chamber. Majority Leader Wright described the job in the following terms:

It's part parish priest – you have to keep peace in the flock; part evangelist – you must go out and try to convert the unconverted; and part prophet – you have to persuade reluctant colleagues that you can see down the road and divine the wisdom of an appropriate course of action.[20]

In short, the majority leader's role is that of co-ordinator. Not only must he attempt to ensure that the disparate elements of the house are working together, but also see that there is some co-ordination between the legislature and the White House.[21]

The role of the minority leader is very similar to that of the majority leader. Like his counterpart he must consult with leading members of his party, particularly the ranking minority members of the committees, and encourage them to act in accordance with agreed party positions. If his party occupies the White House, he is likely to assume the role of the President's chief spokesman in the House. Unlike the majority leader, however, it is not the task of the minority leader to schedule legislation. Nor can the minority leader depend upon the Speaker to use the chamber's rules to bolster his persuasive abilities. In fact, the power of the minority leader is derived mainly from being at the centre of an important information network in the House, though as chairman of his party's committee on committees he may be able to obtain a prestigious committee slot as a reward for a loyal supporter. The Speaker has also tended to accept the minority leader's recommendations when filling special, select and joint committees.[22]

Whips and Other Party Offices

Providing support for the Speaker and the leaders of both parties is an extended leadership structure composed of the whip system and a number of party committees. The first whip was appointed in 1897 to help the Speaker further party discipline and encourage attendance at votes.[23] Since then the whip system has expanded in both size and function. Both parties have extended their whip systems to include a number of deputy, at-large, regional and assistant whips as they have sought to broaden the leadership structure and to provide the resources to cope with the proliferation of subcommittees and legislative service organizations.[24] Within the Democratic party, for example, the number of at-large whips increased from three in 1975 to fifteen in 1984.[25] As a further concession to the more independently minded junior members of the House the Democratic caucus agreed to rule changes for the 100th Congress (1987–8) which provided for the election of the majority whip. Prior to this change the whip had, in theory, been appointed by the majority leader, though in practice the choice of the Speaker prevailed.

Recent developments have seen a change in the function of the whip system as the leadership has sought to adapt to the changing institutional environment. The whip's office has become a major source of information for members. 'Whip packets' and 'whip advisories' giving details of legislation and forthcoming votes are often distributed to junior representatives.[26] In return, the whips seek to gather information which may be of use to the Speaker and majority leader when deciding upon a legislative strategy. They will carry out a poll of members to determine the likely reaction to a proposal, and thus provide the leaders with information which enables them to decide whether to bring a bill to the floor, delay for a while or abandon the proposal. With their vital role as both collectors and disseminators of information, the whips are an important component of the leadership structure.

Beginning in the 95th Congress (1977–8), Speaker Tip O'Neill supplemented the Democratic whip system by appointing *task forces* to deal with controversial measures in a strategy described as 'leadership by inclusion'.[27] On one level, the purpose of these task forces was to act like whips: collecting information and asking for a commitment to vote for a specific measure. On another level, they were used to bring junior members into the decision-making process in an attempt to make them more responsive to the demands of the party. The task forces, therefore, were designed both to foster the building of short-term coalitions around a proposal, and to inculcate new members of the majority party with party norms.[28] They were seen as a means of adapting the leadership structure to cope with an institutional environment where individual rights were stressed at the expense of collective norms.

A further opportunity for junior members to be included within the leadership structure is provided by the party committees. By far the most important of these committees are the caucuses or conferences composed of all members of each party. Used for most of the twentieth century merely to nominate a candidate for the speakership and ratify committee assignments, both the Democratic caucus and the Republican Conference have in recent years played a more active role in determining questions of party and committee reorganization. It was the Democratic caucus, for example, which was responsible for transforming the House into a more open and accountable institution during the 1970s. Rule changes agreed by the caucus made the committee chairmen subject to election by a secret ballot, changed committee assignment practices, opened the committees to public scrutiny and gave the subcommittees more independence.[29] The caucuses have also devoted attention, on occasion, to substantive as well as procedural issues. In 1972 the Democratic caucus forced a House vote on a non-binding resolution to end the Vietnam War. During the Carter Administration it approved a resolution blocking a proposed increase in employees' social security contributions, and then voted to oppose Administration plans to end federal controls on the price of oil.

Generally speaking, the caucuses' forays into the policy-making arena have not been successful, partly because they have been seen as usurping the powers of the standing committees, but also because individual members have no wish to be bound by a decision of the caucus. For similar reasons, the so-called Policy Committees of both parties have tended to provide the leadership with assistance on legislative scheduling rather than determining comprehensive partisan positions.[30] As a result of being an almost permanent minority party since 1932, and consequently denied the resources available to the majority, the Republicans established a Research Committee to conduct research and policy analysis for the party. Both parties also have campaign committees called the Democratic Congressional Campaign Committee (DCCC) and the National Republican Congressional Committee (NRCC). The purpose of these committees is to promote the election of Democrats and Republicans.[31]

The expansion of the whip system, the development of task forces, and the increase in the scope of the party committees means that leadership in the modern House involves, at one level or the other, almost every representative. As individualism has become the prevailing norm, so the leadership structure has developed accordingly. At the apex of this structure, however, remains the Speaker. Although constrained by the overall institutional context in which he operates, the resources of the office are still sufficient to allow a strong personality to impose his will on the House. Evidence of this can be seen in the actions of Speaker Wright.

Speaker Wright

The technique of bringing more members into the leadership circle was abandoned by Jim Wright when he was elected Speaker at the beginning of the 100th Congress (1987–8). Taking advantage of his position as the most senior elected Democrat in the country, Wright sought to transform the speakership from a consensus builder and power broker to an agenda setter and power wielder. In addition to highly publicized policy initiatives on Nicaragua and taxation, which challenged the position of the Reagan Administration, Wright made greater use of his institutional resources to impose his will upon the House. As Majority Leader Thomas S. Foley (Democrat, Washington) has remarked: 'This Speaker is not diffident or embarrassed about the power of the speakership.'[32] In particular, Wright has used his position as chairman of the Democratic Steering and Policy Committee to exercise control over committee assignments. In 1987, for example, he backed the nomination of Representative Lindsay Thomas (Democrat, Georgia) to the Appropriations Committee. The Speaker's influence was acknowledged by Representative Thomas, who declared: 'The Speaker is the reason I'm on that committee, and Thomas doesn't forget it.'[33] Second, Wright has used his control over the Rules Committee, derived from his right to appoint its Democratic members, to regulate the flow of legislation to the floor. He has also relied upon the Rules Committee to restrict the opportunity for amending legislation from the floor.[34]

The power and prestige of the Speaker has undoubtedly been enhanced under Jim Wright. Whether such an authoritarian manner can persist, however, must be open to question. The basic institutional context in which the Speaker must now operate would seem to preclude any sustained dominance by one individual, no matter how powerful they may appear. Speaker Wright's power would seem to rest largely upon the perception that he has been successful in promoting the interests of both the Democratic party and Democratic representatives. If that perception should change, then there would certainly be calls for a change in leadership style. As one liberal Democrat noted when referring to Speaker Wright: 'It's like Evel Knievel. As long as you keep jumping over all the cars, it's OK. But if you miss one it could be costly.'[35]

THE US SENATE

The Presiding Officer

In the Senate there is no institutional or party official comparable in power and prestige to the Speaker of the House of Representatives. The Constitution's only reference to leadership posts and responsibilities in the Senate are contained in two passages of Article I, Section 3. One clause provides that the Vice-President of the United States 'shall be President of the Senate, but shall have no vote, unless they are equally divided'. The other provides that the 'Senate shall .. choose . . . a President *pro tempore*, in the absence of the Vice-President, or when he shall exercise the office of President of the United States'. Since 1945 the practice has been for the longest serving member of the majority party to assume the office of President *Pro Tempore*. Although either the Vice-President or the President *Pro Tempore* may preside over the Senate, the role of presiding officer is normally left to a few junior members of the majority party, who usually take turns to serve thirty minutes each in the chair. Figure 11.2 sets out the leadership structure of the US Senate in the 100th Congress.

On a few occasions during the nineteenth century the President *Pro Tempore* was authorized to appoint members of the Senate to standing committees but, generally, senators have been reluctant to place substantial power in the hands of the presiding officer. The official powers of the President *Pro Tempore* include the right to recognize members wishing to speak, to decide points of order subject to approval by the full Senate, and to appoint senators to House-Senate conferences and special committees. There have been times when rulings by the Vice-President or President *Pro Tempore* on points of order have had a significant impact. For example, Senator Arthur Vandenberg's (Republican, Michigan) ruling in 1948 that a procedural motion was not a pending measure, and therefore not subject to the cloture requirements of Rule 22, made it impossible to end filibusters against Civil Rights legislation. Similarly, the tie-breaking vote possessed by the Vice-President has, at times, proved to be important. It would be a mistake, however, to confuse either office with that of the Speaker.

Floor Leaders

Rather than being concentrated in the hands of the presiding officers, power in the Senate has tended to be entrusted to the majority and minority leaders since the early twentieth century. A lack of constitutional authority, and the fact that senators tend to regard themselves as unregimented ambassadors from their states, however, has severely limited the power of

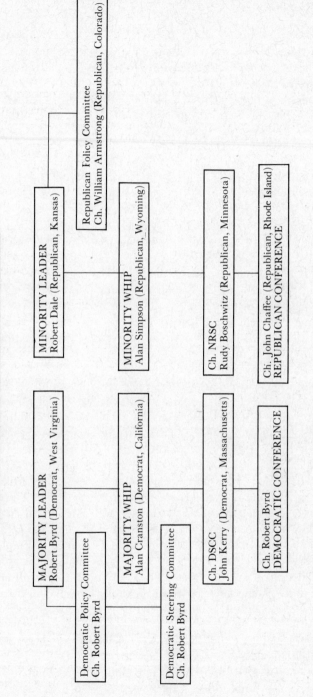

PRESIDING OFFICER
Vice-President, George Bush
President Pro Tempore, John Stennis (Democrat, Mississippi)

MINORITY LEADER
Robert Dale (Republican, Kansas)

Republican Policy Committee
Ch. William Armstrong (Republican, Colorado)

MINORITY WHIP
Alan Simpson (Republican, Wyoming)

Ch. NRSC
Rudy Boschwitz (Republican, Minnesota)

Ch. John Chaffee (Republican, Rhode Island)
REPUBLICAN CONFERENCE

MAJORITY LEADER
Robert Byrd (Democrat, West Virginia)

Democratic Policy Committee
Ch. Robert Byrd

MAJORITY WHIP
Alan Cranston (Democrat, California)

Democratic Steering Committee
Ch. Robert Byrd

Ch. DSCC
John Kerry (Democrat, Massachusetts)

Ch. Robert Byrd
DEMOCRATIC CONFERENCE

Figure 11.2 *The leadership structure of the Senate, 100th Congress. (Adapted from Roger H. Davidson and Walter J. Oleszek* Congress and its Members, *p. 186)*

the party leadership. As Lord Bryce noted in 1891: 'No senator can be said to have any authority beyond that of exceptional talent and experience.'[36] More recently, Senator George J. Mitchell (Democrat, Maine) has remarked that: 'It states the obvious to say that the job of leadership is difficult in a body composed of 100 individuals.'[37] Individual leaders such as John W. Kern (Democrat, Indiana) between 1911 and 1917, Joseph T. Robinson (Democrat, Arkansas) between 1933 and 1937 and Lyndon B. Johnson (Democrat, Texas) between 1955 and 1961, have managed to exert considerable authority, but such power has been personal rather than institutional. This point was expressed by Johnson in an interview in 1960: 'There is no patronage; no power to discipline; no authority to fire senators like a President can fire members of his cabinet . . . the only real power available to the leader is the power of persuasion.'[38] Johnson's skill as a leader lay in a willingness to use the full resources of his office for persuasion in what became known as the 'Johnson Treatment'.[39] Robert Byrd (Democrat, West Virginia), majority leader from 1977 to 1980, and from 1987 to 1988, concurred with Johnson's view of the office. He told the Senate that being majority leader was a more onerous task than being President of the United States because: 'It is extremely difficult to deal with the wishes and needs of ninety-nine other senators ... and I cannot fire any of them.'[40]

In general, party leadership in the Senate has tended to be collegial in nature with the leader needing to co-operate with committee chairmen and individual senators. This has meant that the pattern of leadership in the chamber has reflected changes in the Senate's membership, committee structure, norms and rules.[41] The change in the style of leadership from the 1950s to the 1980s, for example, reflected the altered environment of the Senate: from a largely southern-dominated, senior-controlled, committee-centred institution to a much more egalitarian institution. Mike Mansfield (Democrat, Montana), majority leader from 1961 to 1977, viewed his position as one among equals: 'I can see a Senate of real egalitarianism, the decline of seniority as a major factor, and the new senators being seen and heard and not being wallflowers' he commented.[42] Emphasizing the difference between his leadership style and that of Lyndon Johnson, Mansfield stated: 'I never twisted arms. My predecessor did and gathered chits. I didn't know how. But even if I did, I might have lost down the road because people who have their arms twisted are less co-operative later.'[43]

The problem faced by Senator Mansfield, his successor Robert Byrd, and the Republicans Howard Baker (Republican, Tennessee), majority leader between 1981 and 1984, and Bob Dole (Republican, Kansas), majority leader from 1985 to 1986, was how to organize a chamber in which individual prerogatives are stressed. Senator Byrd's technique was to use his unsurpassed knowledge of the Senate's rules to advance his party's legislative programme. Senator Baker, on the other hand, worked assiduously to be accommodating, always searching for a compromise position. Comparing Baker with Senator Dole, his successor as majority leader, Senator Max Baucus (Democrat, Montana) reported that: 'Baker was more polished, more accommodating, more amiable. He paid more attention to comity. Dole is more assertive, more aggressive. Not quite as patient.'[44] As Baucus intimates, Senator Dole's style of leadership was more prominent than Baker's. He was a leader more in the tradition of Lyndon Johnson than Mike Mansfield.

Implicit in the different leadership styles of recent majority leaders is the idea that the office's lack of institutional power means that great emphasis is placed upon personal qualities of leadership. The only parliamentary power which the majority leader possesses is the right to be recognized first in debates. Although this right of prior recognition has occasionally allowed the majority and minority leaders to exercise some control over debate, the power of the leadership is more generally derived from the fact that it is at the centre of communications in the Senate. Responsible for scheduling legislation, leaders have an unsurpassed knowledge of both the legislative agenda and the wishes of individual senators. It was this power 'to help or hinder' that Lyndon Johnson was so adept at using.

In theory, a Democratic leader, as chairman of the Democratic caucus, Steering Committee and Policy Committee, has access to greater *potential* power than his Republican counterpart, who chairs no other party committee. The advantage of the Democratic form of leadership is that it provides the leader with greater staff resources and authority. The main virtue of the Republican form of corporate leadership, where the top leadership posts are held by different senators, is that it facilitates greater participation in the affairs of the party. In an environment where individualism is stressed, the more inclusive nature of the Republican leadership structure may be important.

Whips and Other Party Offices

The posts of majority and minority whip were first established in the Senate in the early twentieth century.[45] Since then, both offices have evolved to perform much the same function as the whip system in the House of Representatives, though with less success. As the Senate is a smaller institution than the House, the two floor leaders have not deemed it necessary to delegate power to their whips. Instead, they have tended to perform the whip's role of collecting and disseminating information themselves. On those occasions when the whips have become major figures in the party, their prominence has largely been due to their own political prowess, and not the result of any institutional prestige.[46]

Similarly, the party caucuses in the Senate have not played quite as prominent a role in reforming the procedures of the chamber as that performed by the Democratic caucus in the House. For most of the twentieth century both the Senate Democratic caucus and the Republican Conference met only to elect party leaders and approve committee assignments. Lyndon Johnson when majority leader, for example, was quite happy to allow the Democratic caucus to lie dormant. In his heyday, the caucus 'would be convened just once or twice during the session, usually to hear the majority leader's State-of-the-Union message or some similar Johnsonian pronouncement'.[47] With an independent chairman the Republican Conference is less dependent upon the proclivities of the floor leader, and as a result, has tended to meet more regularly than its Democratic counterpart. Under the leadership of Senator James McClure (Republican, Idaho), who was chairman between 1979 and 1984, the Conference devoted most of its resources to providing the media with information about the accomplishments of Republican senators.[48] In contrast, the Democrats have left the responsibility for publicizing the activities of the party to the Democratic Senatorial Campaign Committee (DSCC). Both the DSCC and the National Republican Senatorial Committee (NRSC) also provide campaign assistance to their respective candidates.

In addition to panels which assign party members to committees, known as the Committee on Committees in the case of the Republicans, and the Steering Committee in the case of the Democrats, both parties also have policy committees. Established by a provision of the Legislative Appropriations Act (1947) the purpose of these committees is to provide advice when a party is in the majority, and to recommend party positions when a party is in the minority. The fact that the Democratic Policy Committee is chaired by the floor leader has meant that the committee has tended to act as an arm of the leadership. In contrast, the Republican Policy Committee has long provided research assistance to individual Republican senators to counter the advantage in resources that the Democrats have normally possessed as the majority party. It should be stressed, however, that both committees are misnamed. Although they have occasionally investigated and considered alternatives to initiatives from the US President, neither has ever put forward an overall congressional party programme.[49] The decentralization and fragmentation of power in the Senate is so well established that few senators are willing to place power in the hands of a policy committee.

PARTY LEADERSHIP IN CONGRESS

Despite the wide range of resources at their command, party leaders in both the House and the Senate cannot order their colleagues to toe the party line. Their ability to meet their responsibilities, therefore, depends upon their persuasive capabilities, their success in manipulating their resources to influence the scheduling of legislation, filling of committee places and provision of favours. The success of these techniques will depend upon the demands and attitudes of individual members of Congress. Recent developments, which have seen the influx of a more independent generation of congressmen possessing considerable personal resources, have made the task of leadership more difficult. As Majority Leader Byrd has observed:

Going back to my earliest years in the Senate, I think there was more of an allegiance to party, more of an establishment-minded feeling. There was more cohesiveness on the part of political parties than there has been in recent years. The emergence of the 'individual' has been a kind of phenomenon.[50]

This is yet more evidence of the way in which membership changes generate institutional change. Changes in Congress's membership have led leaders to reassess their strategies and functions. As a result, although it is important to note that the two parties still organize Congress, ascriptions of party government in Congress would seem to be less appropriate than ever.

Notes

1 Alexander Hamilton *Federalist* (1) in Alexander Hamilton, James Madison and John Jay *The Federalist Papers* ed. Max Beloff (Oxford, Basil Blackwell, 1987), p. 2.
2 See Mary P. Follett *The Speaker of the House of Representatives* (New York, Burt Franklin, 1974, Reprint of 1902 ed), pp. 25–6.
3 Speakers of the House of Commons have not always been non-partisan. Modern standards of impartiality were only really established with Speaker Lefevre (1839–57).
4 Follett *The Speaker*, p. 64.
5 For the origins of the American party system see Ronald P. Formisano 'Deferential-Participant Politics: The early Republic's Political Culture, 1789–1840' *American Political Science Review* (June), 1974, pp. 473–87; Richard Hofstadter *The Idea of a Party System* (Berkeley, University of California Press, 1969); William Chambers *Political Parties in the New Nation* (Oxford, Oxford University Press, 1963) and Joseph Charles *The Origins of the American Party System* (New York, Harper and Row, 1956).
6 The only other person to have been elected Speaker during his first term in the House of Representatives was William Pennington (Whig, New Jersey) in 1859.

7 For a sympathetic account of Henry Clay's term as Speaker see Hurburt Bruce Fuller *The Speaker of the House* (Boston, Little, Brown, 1909), p. 58; Ralph V. Harlow *The History of Legislative Methods in the Period Before 1825* (New Haven, Yale University Press, 1917), p. 208 and Follett *The Speaker*, p. 79. A less sympathetic account, suggesting that Clay's power has been exaggerated, is to be found in James Sterling Young *The Washington Community 1800–1825* (New York, Columbia University Press, 1966), pp. 131–5.

8 Quoted in Follett *The Speaker*, p. 288.

9 Neil MacNeil *Forge of Democracy* (New York, David McKay, 1963), pp. 71–2.

10 Prior to 1839 the Speaker had been chosen by a secret ballot of the entire House.

11 MacNeil *Forge of Democracy*, p. 79.

12 For details of these procedures see ch. 10, pp. 223–6.

13 Barbara Sinclair *Majority Leadership in the US House* (Baltimore, John Hopkins University Press, 1983), p. 32.

14 Joseph Cooper and David Brady 'Institutional Context and Leadership Style: The House from Cannon to Rayburn' *American Political Science Review* (June), 1981, p. 423.

15 Barbara Sinclair 'Majority Party Leadership Strategies For Coping With the New US House' *Legislative Studies Quarterly* (August), 1981, p. 394.

16 George Galloway *History of the United States House of Representatives* (New York, Thomas Y. Crowell, 1961), p. 211.

17 Robert L. Peabody *Leadership in Congress* (Boston, Little, Brown, 1976), p. 34.

18 Ibid.

19 James Wright quoted in Sinclair *Majority Leadership in the US House*, p. 41.

20 *New York Times*, 13 March 1984, p. B6.

21 See Randall B. Ripley *Party Leaders in the House of Representatives* (Washington DC, Brookings, 1967), pp. 54–80.

22 For a discussion of the role of the minority party see Charles O. Jones *The Minority Party in Congress* (Boston, Little, Brown, 1970).

23 For the origins of the whips see Randall B. Ripley 'The Party Whip Organisations in the United States House of Representatives' *American Political Science Review* (September), 1964, pp. 561–76 and Lawrence C. Dodd and Terry Sullivan 'Majority Party Leadership and Partisan Vote Gathering: The House Democratic Whip System' in Frank H. Mackaman ed. *Understanding Congressional Leadership* (Washington DC, Congressional Quarterly Press, 1981), pp. 227–60.

24 For a discussion of this development see Sinclair *Majority Leadership in the US House*, pp. 55–67.

25 Burdette A. Loomis 'Congressional Careers and Party Leadership in the Contemporary House of Representaatives' *American Journal of Political Science* (February), 1984, p. 187.

26 Sinclair 'Majority Party Leadership Strategies', pp. 394–5.

27 Barbara Sinclair 'The Speaker's Task Force in the Post-Reform House of Representatives' *American Political Science Review* (June), 1981, pp. 397–410.

28 James C. Garrand and Kathleen M. Clayton 'Socialization to Partisanship in

the US House: The Speaker's Task Force' *Legislative Studies Quarterly* (August), 1986, pp. 409–28.

29 See ch. 9 for details of these changes.

30 See Charles O. Jones *Party and Policy-Making: The House Republican Policy Committee* (New Brunswick, Rutgers University Press, 1964).

31 For details of the activities of these committees see ch. 4 pp. 75–9.

32 *Congressional Quarterly Weekly Report*, 12 March 1988, p. 623.

33 Ibid., p. 624.

34 See ch. 10, pp. 229–31.

35 *Congressional Quarterly Weekly Report*, 12 March 1988, p. 625. Evel Knievel was a stunt motorcyclist who achieved fame by jumping his motorcycle over buses.

36 James Bryce *The American Commonwealth* (London, Macmillan, 1891), p. 202.

37 *Congressional Quarterly Weekly Report*, 16 April 1988, p. 976.

38 *US New and World Report*, 7 June 1960, p. 88.

39 For a description of 'the treatment' see Rowland Evans and Robert Novak *Lyndon B. Johnson: The Exercise of Power* (New York, New American Library, 1966), p. 104.

40 *Congressional Record* 96th Congress, 2nd sess., 18 April 1980, p. S3924.

41 See Norman J. Ornstein, Robert L. Peabody and David W. Rohde 'The Contemporary Senate: Into the 1980s' in Lawrence C. Dodd and Bruce I. Oppenheimer eds *Congress Reconsidered* (Washington DC, Congressional Quarterly Press, 1981), p. 20.

42 *National Journal*, 25 December 1976, p. 1803.

43 Quoted in David M. Abshire and Ralph D. Nurnberger eds *The Growing Power of Congress* (Beverley Hills, Sage, 1981), p. 161.

44 *Congressional Quarterly Weekly Report*, 29 June 1985, p. 1270.

45 See Walter J. Oleszek 'Party Whips in the United States Senate' *Journal of Politics* (November), 1971, p. 1270.

46 Randall B. Ripley *Power in the Senate* (New York, St. Martin's Press, 1969), p. 35.

47 US Senate, Temporary Select Committee to Study the Senate Committee System, 'Operation of the Senate Committee System' *appendix to the Second Report* John G. Stewart 'Committee System Management: Getting the Act Together – The Senate Leadership's Role in the Policy Process' 1977, p. 7.

48 For further details see ch. 4, p. 76.

49 See Hugh A. Bone 'An Introduction to the Senate Policy Committees' *American Political Science Review*, (June), 1956, pp. 339–59 and Hugh A. Bone *Party Committees and National Politics* (Seattle, University of Washington Press, 1958).

50 *Congressional Quarterly Weekly Report*, 9 May 1981, p. 786.

12

The Contemporary Congress

There can be little doubt that Congress has been transformed over the last two decades. In terms of their procedures, workload and membership, both the House of Representatives and the Senate have experienced considerable change. What is open to doubt, however, is the extent to which these changes have *improved* Congress and enhanced its position in the American system of government. Dissatisfaction with Congress's performance continues to be expressed from both within and outside the institution. Typical is Senator Dale Bumper's (Democrat, Arkansas) assertion that: 'Unless we recognize that things are out of control and procedures have to be changed, we'll never be an effective legislative body again.'[1] Despite all the efforts of the reform movement of the 1970s there is still concern that the contemporary Congress is failing to perform effectively.

In many respects the concern about congressional performance being expressed by Senator Bumper is nothing new. Woodrow Wilson once described the House of Representatives as 'a disintegrated mass of jarring elements'.[2] What is new is the sense that Congress is not just inefficient but incapable of meeting the demands of modern American society. Such concerns pose real questions about the role that a legislature is able to perform in a society with complex, rapidly changing problems. Like legislatures throughout the western world Congress is faced with the problem of adapting to an environment in which there seems to be little time for the slow, detailed, consideration of public policy. Seemingly incapable both of assimilating vast quantities of information and of formulating coherent policy responses, Congress like other western legislatures, has become reliant upon the Executive and bureaucracies for legislative initiatives. In many cases it has even delegated legislative authority to these other bodies.

Many of the reforms of Congress's procedures which occurred during the 1970s were characterized as attempts to reassert the legislature's role in American government. Despite their packaging, however, the main purpose of these changes was to further personal prerogatives rather than to improve institutional efficiency. Instead of making Congress more efficient the reforms, on the whole, increased the power and resources of individual senators and representatives. They have been given more staff and greater access to the policy-making process. The result has been a dispersal of power which has tended to undermine the authority of party and committee leaders, thereby making it even more difficult to formulate and pass coherent public policy. Nowhere has this development been more evident than in Congress's inability to deal with the budget deficit. Unwilling either to raise taxes or cut government spending for fear of harming their constituents, members of Congress simply abrogated their policy-making responsibilities by passing the Balanced Budget and Emergency Deficit Control Act (1985), commonly called the Gramm-Rudman-Hollings Act. Under the terms of this act a procedure was established to implement automatic cuts in government spending to produce a balanced budget by 1991.[3]

The difficulties experienced by Congress in its attempts to find a solution to the problem of the budget deficit are indicative of the obstacles facing the legislature when it tries to address *national* issues. Not only are there problems in collecting and assimilating information on such a complex subject, but the concern shown by individual senators and representatives for the welfare of their constituents makes it extremely difficult to find agreement for a national policy. Parochial interests tend to take precedence over national interests. After all, the size of the national debt is a meaningless abstraction to most constituents; the level of welfare payments and the size of the tax bill are not. Such parochialism means that the only real way in which the national policy can emerge in Congress is through the summation of local issues. Although it could be argued that this is, in fact, the only way in which national interest can be defined in a country as large and diverse as the United States, the resulting policy tends to be vague and incoherent, necessarily the consequence of compromise.

In recent years members of Congress have become even more preoccupied with parochial interests as changes in the electoral environment have emphasized the need to respond to the demands of constituents. The perception that members ignore their constituents at the risk of electoral defeat has led to a general reordering of congressional priorities. Learning from what are believed to be the mistakes of defeated members, both representatives and senators are paying more attention to their constituencies. Both time and resources have been switched from legislative-orientated to constituency-orientated activities. It is not too much of an exaggeration to suggest that many members of Congress now behave more in the manner of ombudsmen than legislators. They spend much of their time responding to requests from constituents to sort out problems, provide information or simply give advice.

Such developments have made a mockery of Congress's attempts to become less dependent upon the President and the bureaucracy for policy initiatives. Unable to produce coherent programmes of their own, members of Congress are just as dependent as ever upon the Executive Branch for answers to America's problems.

In addition to reinforcing the difficulties Congress experiences when trying to act in the national interest, the increased emphasis on the provision of constituency services has also had an impact upon the congressional power structure.[4] Although the basic committee structure of Congress has remained unchanged since 1977, the personal machines which representatives and senators have built to facilitate communications with their constituents have enabled them to assert their independence from party or committee ties. Each member of Congress is effectively the head of a legislative enterprise, commanding the freedom and resources to pursue his or her own interests regardless of the collective good. Some commentators have even suggested that it is time to reassess the way in which the power structure within Congress has traditionally been described.[5]

Most studies of the organization of Congress tend to concentrate on the formal structural units of committees, subcommittees, party caucuses and leadership posts. Each member of Congress is described in terms of his or her membership of these units and his or her behaviour analysed accordingly. The emergence of personal political machines, however, means that it might be useful to augment such an approach with one which recognizes the new circumstances. In effect, members of Congress should be viewed as being at the centre of a legislative enterprise which cuts across the formal boundaries of the traditional structural units. Not only have legislators forged links with Political Action Committees to further their chances of re-election, but reforms have also provided them with their own staff on committees. They thus control personal resources which reach out beyond their constituencies into congressional committees and interest groups. The recruitment of congressional staff by the Executive Branch and federal agencies merely adds to the legislator's sphere of influence. In other words, the individual representative or senator is surrounded by a network of personal and committee staff and 'alumni' working elsewhere in Washington DC. This network provides the member of Congress with information, legislative resources and a power base which is quite independent of the formal structure of Congress.

Although it would be unwise to dismiss the importance of the traditional structural units within Congress, it is important to note the emergence of personal political machines. Not only have they contributed to the atomization of power within the Senate and the House of Representatives, and made it more difficult to ensure coherence, but they have also institutionalized the link between the legislator and his or her constituency. Two conclusions about the contemporary Congress seem to follow inexorably from these observations. First, Congress is better described as a collection of legislators rather than a legislature. Second, Congress is first and foremost a representative institution. Representation of the people has been achieved at the expense of law-making capacity. As a representative institution Congress reflects the fragmentation of American society.

Notes

1 *Congressional Quarterly Weekly Report*, 3 January 1987, p. 4.
2 Woodrow Wilson *Congressional Government* (London, Constable, 1914), p. 210.
3 The Balanced Budget and Emergency Deficit Control Act (1985) was amended in 1987 to make 1994 the target year for a balanced budget.
4 Much of the discussion which follows is taken from Christopher J. Bailey 'Beyond the New Congress: Aspects of Congressional Development in the 1980s' *Parliamentary Affairs* (April), 1988, pp. 244–6.
5 See R.H. Salisbury and K.A. Shepsle 'US Congressman as Enterprise' *Legislative Studies Quarterly* (November), 1981, pp. 559–76.

Select Bibliography

So much has been written about Congress that this bibliography must be selective and concentrate in the main upon recent authoritative books on the subject. Neither essays within collected works nor articles have been included for reasons of space, though both are, of course, invaluable for keeping track of recent developments in the study of Congress. Further sources of material on Congress include the *Congressional Directories, the Almanac of American Politics, Congressional Quarterly Weekly Report* and the *National Journal*.

Abshire, David M. and Nurnberger, Ralph D. eds *The Growing Power of Congress* (Beverley Hills, Sage, 1981)

Alexander, DeAlva Stanwood *History and Procedure of the House of Representatives* (Boston, Houghton Mifflin, 1916)

Alexander, Herbert E. *Financing Politics* (Washington DC, Congressional Quarterly Press, 1984)

Arnold, R. Douglas *Congress and the Bureaucracy* (New Haven, Yale University Press, 1979)

Aydelotte, William O. ed. *The History of Parliamentary Behaviour* (Princeton, Princeton University Press, 1977)

Bailey, Christopher J. *The Republican Party in the US Senate 1974–1984* (Manchester, Manchester University Press, 1988)

Bibby, John F. and Davidson, Roger H. *On Capitol Hill* (New York, Hall, Rinehart and Winston, 1967)

Bolling, Richard *Power in the House* (New York, Capricorn, 1974)

Bowles, Nigel *The White House and Capitol Hill* (Oxford, Clarendon Press, 1987)

Brady, David W. *Congressional Voting in a Partisan Era* (Kansas, University of Kansas Press, 1973)

Brown, George Rothwell *The Leadership of Congress* (Indianapolis, Bobbs-Merrill, 1922)

Bryce, James *The American Commonwealth* (London, Macmillan, 1891)

Burdette, Franklin L. *Filibustering in the Senate* (Princeton, Princeton University Press, 1940)

Chamberlain, Lawrence *The President, Congress, and Legislation* (New York, Columbia University Press, 1946)

Clapp, Charles L. *The Congressman* (New York, Doubleday, 1963)

Clark, Joseph S. *Congress: The Sapless Branch* (New York, Harper and Row, 1964)

Crabb, Cecil V. and Holt, Pat M. *Invitation to Struggle: Congress, the President, and Foreign Policy* (Washington DC, Congressional Quarterly Press, 1984)

Davidson, Roger H. *The Role of the Congressman* (Indianapolis, Bobbs-Merrill, 1969)

Davidson, Roger H. and Oleszek, Walter J. *Congress and its Members* (Washington DC, Congressional Quarterly Press, 1985)

Dodd, Lawrence C. and Schott, Richard L. *Congress and the Administrative State* (New York, John Wiley, 1979)

Dodd, Lawrence C. and Oppenheimer, Bruce I. eds *Congress Reconsidered* (Washington DC, Congressional Quarterly Press, 1985 edn)

Edwards, George *Presidential Influence in Congress* (San Francisco, W.H. Freeman, 1980)

Fenno, Richard F. *Congressmen in Committees* (Boston, Little, Brown, 1973)

——*Home Style* (Boston, Little, Brown, 1977)

——*The United States Senate: A Bicameral Perspective* (Washington DC, American Enterprise Institute, 1982)

Fiorina, Morris P. *Congress: Keystone of the Washington Establishment* (New Haven, Yale University Press, 1977)

Fisher, Louis *Constitutional Conflicts Between Congress and the President* (Princeton, Princeton University Press, 1985)

Foley, Michael *The New Senate* (New Haven, Yale University Press, 1980)

Follett, Mary P. *The Speaker of the House of Representatives* (New York, Burt Franklin, 1974. Reprint of 1902 edition)

Fox, Harrison W. and Hammond, Susan Webb *Congressional Staffs* (New York, Free Press, 1977)

Frank, Thomas and Weisband, Edward *Foreign Policy by Congress* (Oxford, Oxford University Press, 1979)

Fuller, Huburt Bruce *The Speaker of the House* (Boston, Little, Brown, 1909)

Galloway, George *The Legislative Process in Congress* (New York, Thomas Y. Crowell, 1953)

——*History of the United States House of Representatives* (New York, Thomas Y. Crowell, 1961)

Gertzoy, Irwin N. *Congressional Women* (New York, Praeger, 1984)

Goldenberg, Edie N. and Traugott, Michael W. *Campaigning for Congress*

(Washington DC, Congressional Quarterly Press, 1984)

Hale, Dennis ed. *The United States Congress* (Chestnut Hill, Mass., Boston College, 1982)

Hamilton, Alexander, Madison, James and Jay, John *The Federalist Papers* ed. Max Beloff (Oxford, Basil Blackwell, 1987)

Hamilton, James *The Power to Probe* (New York, Random House, 1976)

Harlow, Ralph V. *The History of Legislative Methods in the Period Before 1825* (New Haven, Yale University Press, 1917)

Haynes, George H. *The Senate of the United States* 2 vols (Boston, Houghton Mifflin, 1938).

Hershey, Majorie R. *Running for Office* (Chatham, NJ, Chatham House, 1985)

Hibbing, John R. *Choosing to Leave: Voluntary Retirement from the US House of Representatives* (Washington DC, University Press of America, 1982)

Hinckley, Barbara *The Seniority System in Congress* (Bloomington, Indiana University Press, 1970)

——*Congressional Elections* (Washington DC, Congressional Quarterly Press, 1981)

Holt, James *Congressional Insurgents and the Party System 1909–1916* (Cambridge, Mass., Harvard University Press, 1967)

Ippolito, Dennis S. *Congressional Spending* (Ithaca, NY, Cornell University Press, 1981)

Jacobson, Gary C. *Money in Congressional Elections* (New Haven, Yale University Press, 1980)

——*The Politics of Congressional Elections* (Boston, Little, Brown, 1983)

Johannes, John R. *To Serve the People: Congress and Constituency Service* (Lincoln, University of Nebraska Press, 1984)

Jones, Charles O. *Party and Policy-Making: The House Republican Policy Committee* (New Brunswick, Rutgers University Press, 1964)

——*Every Second Year* (Washington DC, Brookings, 1967)

——*The Minority Party in Congress* (Boston, Little, Brown, 1970)

Jones, Rochelle and Woll, Peter *The Private World of Congress* (New York, Free Press, 1979)

King, Anthony ed. *Both Ends of the Avenue* (Washington DC, American Enterprise Institute, 1983)

Kingdon, John W. *Congressmen's Voting Decisions* (New York, Harper and Row, 1973)

Kozak, David *Contexts of Congressional Decision Behavior* (Lanham, Md., University Press of America, 1984)

LeLoup, Lance T. *The Fiscal Congress* (Westport, Conn., Greenwood Press, 1980)

Maas, Arthur *Congress and the Common Good* (New York, Basic Books, 1983)

McCown, Ada C. *The Congressional Conference Committee* (New York, Columbia University Press, 1927)

McCubbins, Matthew D. and Sullivan, Terry eds *Congress: Structure and Policy* (Cambridge, Cambridge University Press, 1987)

Mackaman, Frank H. ed. *Understanding Congressional Leadership* (Washington DC, Congressional Quarterly Press, 1981)

MacNeil, Neil *Forge of Democracy* (New York, David McKay, 1963)

Madison, James *The Debates in the Federal Convention of 1787* eds Gaillard Hunt and James Brown Scott (Oxford, Oxford University Press, 1920)

Main, Jackson Turner *The Upper House in Revolutionary America 1763–1788* (Madison, University of Wisconsin Press, 1967)

Malbin, Michael J. *Unelected Representatives* (New York, Basic Books, 1980)

Mann, Thomas E. *Unsafe at Any Margin* (Washington DC, American Enterprise Institute, 1978)

Mann, Thomas E. and Ornstein, Norman J. eds *The New Congress* (Washington DC, American Enterprise Institute, 1981)

Matsanuga, Spark M. and Chen, Ping *Rulemakers of the House* (Urbana, University of Illinois Press, 1976)

Matthews, Donald R. *US Senators and their World* (Chapel Hill, University of North Carolina Press, 1960)

Matthews, Donald R. and Stimson, James A. *Yeas and Nays* (New York, John Wiley, 1975)

Mayhew, David R. *Congress: The Electoral Connection* (New Haven, Yale University Press, 1974)

Miller, Clem *Member of the House* (New York, Charles Scribners, 1962)

Ogul, Morris S. *Congress Oversees the Bureaucracy* (Pittsburgh, University of Pittsburgh Press, 1976)

Oleszek, Walter J. *Congressional Procedures and the Policy Process* (Washington DC, Congressional Quarterly Press, 1984)

Ornstein, Norman J. ed. *Congress in Change* (New York, Praeger, 1975)

——ed. *President and Congress: Assessing Reagan's First Year* (Washington DC, American Enterprise Institute, 1982)

Ornstein, Norman J., Mann, Thomas E., Malbin, Michael J., Schick, Allan and Bibby, John F. eds *Vital Statistics on Congress 1984–1985* (Washington DC, American Enterprise Institute, 1984)

Parker, Glenn R. ed. *Studies of Congress* (Washington DC, Congressional Quarterly Press, 1984)

Patterson, James T. *Congressional Conservatism and the New Deal* (Lexington, University of Kentucky Press, 1967)

Peabody, Robert L. *Leadership in Congress* (Boston, Little, Brown, 1976)

Peabody, Robert L. and Polsby, Nelson W. eds *New Perspectives on the House of Representatives* (Chicago, Rand McNally, 1977 edn)

Rhodes, John R. *The Futile System* (McClean, Va., EPM Publishing, 1976)

Rieselbach, Leroy N. *Congressional Reform* (Washington DC, Congressional Quarterly Press 1986)

Ripley, Randall B. *Party Leaders in the House of Representatives* (Washington DC, Brookings, 1967)

——*Power in the Senate* (New York, St Martin's Press, 1969)

——*Majority Party Leadership in Congress* (Boston, Little, Brown, 1969)

Ripley, Randall B. and Franklin, Grace A. *Congress, the Bureaucracy, and Public Policy* (Homewood, Ill., Dorsey Press, 1984)

Robinson, James A. *The House Rules Committee* (Indianapolis, Bobbs-Merrill, 1963)

Rothman, David J. *Politics and Power: The United States Senate 1869–1901* (Cambridge, Mass., Harvard University Press, 1966)

Rourke, John *Congress and the Presidency in US Foreign Policymaking* (Boulder, Westview, 1983)

Schick, Allan *Congress and Money* (Washington DC, Urban Institute, 1980)

——*Reconciliation and the Congressional Budget Process* (Washington DC, American Enterprise Institute, 1981)

Schneider, Jerrold E. *Ideological Coalitions in the US Congress* (Westport, Conn., Greenwood Press, 1979)

Shelley, Mack C. *The Permanent Majority* (Alabama, University of Alabama Press, 1983)

Sheppard, B.D. *Rethinking Congressional Reform* (Cambridge, Schenkman, 1985)

Shepsle, Kenneth A. *The Giant Jigsaw Puzzle: Democratic Committee Assignments in the Modern House* (Chicago, University of Chicago Press, 1978)

Shuman, H.E. *Politics and the Budget* (Englewood Cliffs, Prentice Hall, 1984)

Sinclair, Barbara *Majority Leadership in the US House* (Baltimore, John Hopkins University Press, 1983)

Smith, Steven S. and Deering, Christopher J. *Committees in Congress* (Washington DC, Congressional Quarterly Press, 1984)

Sullivan, Terry *Procedural Structure: Success and Influence in Congress* (New York, Praeger, 1984)

Sundquist, James L. *The Decline and Resurgence of Congress* (Washington DC, Brookings, 1981)

Tacheron, Donald G. and Udall, Morris K. *The Job of a Congressman* (Indianapolis, Bobbs-Merrill, 1966)

Tocqueville, Alexis de *Democracy in America* (New York, Vintage Books, 1945)

Truman, David B. *The Congressional Party* (New York, John Wiley, 1959)

——ed. *Congress and America's Future* (Englewood Cliffs, Prentice-Hall, 1965)

Unekis, Joseph K. and Rieselbach, Leroy N. *Congressional Committee Politics* (New York, Praeger, 1984)

Vogler, David J. *The Third House* (Evanston, Northwestern University Press, 1971)

Weaver, Warren *Both Your Houses* (New York, Praeger, 1972)

Whalen, Charles W. *The House and Foreign Policy* (Chapel Hill, University of North Carolina Press, 1982)

White, William S. *Citadel* (New York, Harper and Row, 1957)

Wildavsky, Aaron *The Politics of the Budgetary Process* (Boston, Little, Brown, 1984)

Wilson, Woodrow *Constitutional Government in the United States* (New York, Columbia University Press, 1911)

——*Congressional Government* (London, Constable, 1914)

Wright, Gerald C., Rieselbach, Leroy N. and Dodds, Lawrence C. eds *Policy Change in Congress* (New York, Agathon, 1986)

Young, James Sterling *The Washington Community 1800–1828* (New York, Columbia University Press, 1966)

Index